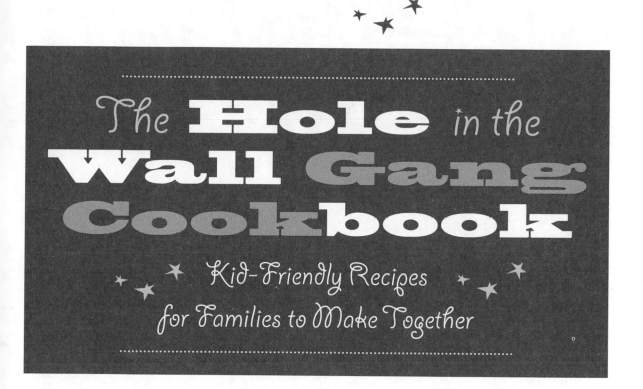

The Hole in the Wall Gang Cookbook

Kid-Friendly Recipes for Families to Make Together

PAUL NEWMAN and **A. E. HOTCHNER**

with the culinary and editorial assistance of
LISA STALVEY and **CAROL WRIGHT**

A FIRESIDE BOOK
PUBLISHED BY SIMON & SCHUSTER

FIRESIDE
Rockefeller Center
1230 Avenue of the Americas
New York, NY 10020

FIRESIDE and colophon are registered trademarks
of Simon & Schuster Inc.

Designed by Songhee Kim

Photos by Janet Durrans appear on pages 10, 21, 22, 37,
43, 47, 51, 52, 65, 77, 82, 96, 113, 115, 119
Photos by Robert Benson appear on pages 12, 17, 60,
84, 92

Manufactured in the United States of America

10   9   8   7   6   5   4   3   2   1

Library of Congress Cataloging-in-Publication Data
Newman, Paul.
    The Hole in the Wall Gang cookbook : kid-friendly
    recipes for families to make together / Paul Newman
    and A. E. Hotchner; with the culinary and editorial
    assistance of Lisa Stalvey and Carol Wright.
        p.   cm.
      "Fireside book."
      Includes index.
      1. Cookery, American.   2. Hole in the Wall Gang
    Camp.   I. Hotchner, A. E.   II. Stalvey, Lisa.   III.
    Wright, Carol.   IV. Title.
    TX715.N5665   1998
    641.5973—dc21   98-35511
                                              CIP

ISBN 0-684-84843-0

Acknowledgments

In assembling this book, Newman and Hotchner cleverly overcame their limited culinary skills by enlisting the invaluable assistance of their indulgent editor, Sydny Miner. They are especially beholden to Lisa Stalvey, Newman's Own food consultant, who contributed her imaginative recipes, and food maven and writer Carol Wright. We also thank Elaine Kaufman for the use of her restaurant.

We dedicate this book to the devoted counselors and staffs of our camps: The Hole in the Wall Gang, Connecticut; The Hole in the Woods Gang, New York state; The Boggy Creek Gang, Florida; The Barretstown Gang, Ireland; the Buffalo Prairie Gang, Illinois; L'Envol, France.

Contents

Preface

I am saddened by the fact that most of the institutions that we cherish in this country—the Congress, the Church, the non-Church, Education, the Bench, Unions, the Press, the White House, Boy Scouts, Marriage, and Apple Pie—are under attack.

Perhaps the least noticed, but the saddest, is the Kitchen.

Young people in the Kitchen.

Young people cooking in the Kitchen.

In a world of fast food, frozen food, and fake food, no blessing could be more welcome than the tumultuous voices of little children piercing the uproar in the kitchen: "Cookie cutter, please!" "Basting brush needed!" "Quick! The spatula!"

It is a sweet song devoutly to be wished.

To this task we have set these pages.

Of the children.

For the children.

By the children.

Nice, huh?

PAUL NEWMAN

Introduction

Fifteen years ago Paul Newman and I half-jokingly started a little salad dressing company. To our amazement it ballooned into a thriving worldwide business, Newman's Own, Inc. At the end of the first year we took one look at the escalating profit sheet and said, Let's give it all away to charities every Christmas, and start every new year from scratch.

Then, in 1987, Newman had the inspiration to build a camp for kids who have cancer, leukemia, and other serious blood diseases. We found a wilderness site in northeastern Connecticut, and Newman set his heart on having the camp in operation for that summer, which meant it had to be built in nine months. By any construction standards it was an impossibility—water, electricity, telephone, septic tanks, cabins, dining hall, gymnasium, boat docks, trails, a stable—in effect, an 1880s mining town right out of *Butch Cassidy.* And yet the impossible became possible. But money alone could never have created the miracle camp that received the first group of sick children in June 1988. Giving—that's what did it; a spontaneous outburst of incredible, selfless, communal giving: building supplies, kitchen equipment, a special swimming pool built by the cooperative efforts of all the Connecticut pool builders, trails and difficult ground work by the Seabees, boats for the pond, a check for $5 million from the Royal Kingdom of Saudi Arabia, a camp teepee from a Sioux chief, medical supplies, construction management—an endless, exhilarating contribution of commodities and services.

These recipes come from Paul Newman and his family, from his friends, and from the winners of the annual Newman's Own–*Good Housekeeping* recipe contest, which awards cash prizes to the winners' designated charities. There are special contest categories for children and for professional food critics.

The cast and crew of the 1996 Hole in the Wall Gang Camp Gala

And then there were the schools; not prompted and not solicited, schools from all over the country, from Hawaii, Alaska, Iowa, New Mexico, began sending the proceeds from walk-a-thons, bike-a-thons, bake-a-thons, bash-a-thons—every conceivable thon except a study-a-thon.

That summer and every summer since, nine hundred children afflicted with cancer and serious blood diseases have had a free ten-day stay at the camp, where, attended by a large staff of devoted counselors, nurses, and doctors, they have swum, ridden horses, fished in the lake, performed in plays, and played tennis, baseball, basketball, and many other sports. There have been children from all over the United States and from England, Germany, Japan, Russia, and France— some on chemotherapy, some in wheelchairs, some who had lost legs and arms, some with exposed catheters. The sounds of laughter and good times belied the fact that these were seriously afflicted children, several of whom would not live to see another summer. To date more than seven thousand children have experienced the joys of the Hole in the Wall Gang Camp.

And now, with our assistance, sister camps have been established in Florida, New York, Illinois, Ireland, and France, all members of the Hole in the Wall Gang Association. At full capacity these six camps will serve 5,225 children annually, and it is projected that a total of 18,300 children will attend these camps from 1997 to the year 2000.

This recipe book is dedicated to those campers and those camps. We have found that most children are fascinated by kitchen activities, and the recipes in this book are designed to give them a good time among the pots, pans, and skillets, either cooking by themselves or helping Mom and Dad cook these delectable dishes.

Last summer when I was at our camp in Connecticut, I ate lunch beside an eight-year-old camper who had never been out of Hartford's rough inner city. I asked him how he liked the food. "Well," he said, "I ate things here that looked sort of yucky, but they sure tasted good going down."

We feel quite sure that children will find these recipes, when cooked, taste very good going down.

A. E. HOTCHNER

On the lake at Ashford

Dear Hole in the Wall,

Throughout my life, many people have asked me about the Hole in the Wall Gang Camp. Especially about its location. And time and time again I've told them, Ashford, Connecticut.

Well, over the years I've found out that what I should have said was there is a campground in Ashford that a lot of kids go to. And as for the location of the camp, I should have said the Hole in the Wall Gang Camp exists just beyond reality, right next to Heaven.

It is a place you can go anytime you want and not be bothered by disease, stress, death, or pain.

What I should have said is that it is an experience. You can't see, hear, touch, or taste it. It exists in our hearts and in our souls.

In short, there is a Hole in the Wall in all of us, and it is a place where we can achieve peace with ourselves and the world.

I should have said it's peace, it's life, and it's magic. It's my Hole in the Wall, and it's my way to freedom.

Ross,
camper

Top Ten Tips for Food and Kitchen Safety

1. Wash your hands early and often. Clean them thoroughly with soap and water before you begin cooking. Wash them again after handling raw meat, poultry, or fish. Wash them before and after you use them to separate or crack eggs, mix dough, or fold in egg whites.

2. Keep cutting boards and work surfaces scrupulously clean. Do not prepare foods that will be eaten raw on surfaces where you have just worked with meat, fish, or poultry.

3. Keep knives and other utensils clean. Don't cut up an apple with an unwashed knife that you have previously used to cut up a chicken.

4. Respect your knives and other sharp tools. Keep them sharp; a dull knife can slip more easily than a sharp one. Keep them in sight; don't leave knives in the bottom of a pan of murky dishwater or under a heap of discarded lettuce leaves.

5. Use common sense when working with electric mixers, food processors, and other powerful kitchen machinery. Young children should have adult supervision when using these tools.

6. Respect the stove. Keep pot handles turned in so that people walking past cannot upset them or small children grab them from below. Do not overfill pots so that they boil over.

7. Remember what is cooking. Stay in the kitchen whenever there is a chance that what is on the stove can get too hot, catch on fire, boil away, or otherwise cause trouble.

8. Wash fruits and vegetables carefully just before you are ready to use them. If you think they have been waxed or sprayed, wash them with a mild detergent and peel them. Unless foods are labeled "organic," they have probably been sprayed with pesticides at some point in their life.

9. Don't let food sit around at room temperature. Bacteria and other microbes thrive on warmth, so keep meats, poultry, fish, eggs, and dairy products in the refrigerator until you are going to cook them. Segregate foods that will be eaten raw from those that must be cooked; don't store raw poultry next to bread or salad greens. Refrigerate leftovers promptly.

10. Cook before you taste. Don't eat globs of raw cookie dough with raw eggs in it. If you want to check the seasoning in your meat loaf, make a tiny patty and cook it in a frying pan. Cook to proper temperatures; salmonella is seriously weakened at 140°F and stopped dead at 160°F.

CHAPTER 1   *Soups and Chilies*

4 QUARTS COLD WATER, PLUS MORE TO
   COVER THE CHICKEN IF NEEDED
1 SMALL WHOLE CHICKEN (THE
   SMALLEST YOU CAN FIND), RINSED
   INSIDE AND OUT WITH COLD WATER
1 BAY LEAF
2 CARROTS
1 BAKING POTATO (IDAHO OR RUSSET)
1 YELLOW ONION
2 STALKS CELERY, CUT INTO ¼-INCH
   SLICES (ABOUT 1 CUP)
SALT AND PEPPER TO TASTE
1 TABLESPOON FRESH THYME, OR
   1 TEASPOON DRIED THYME
10 SODA CRACKERS, CRUMBLED FOR
   GARNISH

*Y*ou can turn Newman's Favorite Chicken Soup *into your own favorite chicken soup by using any of the variations that follow the master recipe or by thinking up your own. When you add the cooked chicken meat to the soup, you can use a lot to make the soup thick and stewy, or just a little to keep it light in texture.*

1. Put the water into a stockpot no smaller than 8 quarts, large enough to hold the chicken comfortably. Add the chicken, bay leaf, and additional water to cover the chicken if necessary.

2. Bring the pot to a boil over high heat, then turn to medium-low. With a spoon or ladle, carefully skim off the grayish scum that rises to the top. Continue skimming every 10 minutes, for as long as 30 minutes, until no more scum appears.

3. Peel the carrots, cut them lengthwise into rectangular logs, and cut the logs crosswise into ½-inch dice. Peel the potato and cut it into ½-inch slices. Cut the slices lengthwise into rectangular logs and cut the logs into ½-inch dice. Cut the onion into pieces about the same size as the carrots and potato.

4. When the chicken is almost done, about 40 to 60 minutes, add the carrots, potato, onion, and celery, and continue simmering until the vegetables are soft, about 10 minutes.

5. When the chicken is done, carefully remove it from the soup with a strainer or tongs. Don't worry if it falls apart. Remove the bay leaf and discard. Turn off the heat.

6. Skim off any excess fat from the top of the soup with a spoon or paper towels.

7. Season the soup carefully with salt and pepper. Stir in the thyme.

8. When the chicken is cool enough to handle, re-

move the skin, pick the meat off the bones, and cut it into bite-sized pieces.

9. Ladle 9 cups of the broth and vegetables into a pan, about 1½ cups of broth per person. Add 1½ cups of cut-up chicken, more or less depending on your personal preference. Reheat the soup. Serve garnished with the crumbled soda crackers.

SERVES 6, WITH LEFTOVERS

VARIATIONS:

Chicken Soup with Rice: Add precooked rice when you heat up the chicken meat with the soup.

Chicken Soup with Pasta: Add precooked pasta when you heat up the chicken meat with the soup. Small pasta shapes, such as macaroni elbows, little shells, orzo (grains), and orecchiette (little ears) are good. So are thin noodles, such as capellini (angel hair), either broken up or whole. If you like your soup chunky, try a larger pasta such as rigatoni.

Chicken Soup with Ginger: When you put the vegetables into the pot, add 1 tablespoon of fresh ginger, peeled and cut into thin matchstick shapes.

Chicken Soup with Beans: Add precooked black beans, white beans, or lima beans when you heat up the chicken meat with the soup.

Newman and friend

Jack and the Beanstalk Soup

For the soup:

ONE 26-OUNCE JAR NEWMAN'S OWN
SOCKAROONI SPAGHETTI SAUCE
(FULL OF ALL THE GOOD THINGS
JACK'S MOTHER WISHED SHE HAD
IN HER GARDEN) OR YOUR
FAVORITE MEATLESS SPAGHETTI
SAUCE

2 CUPS WATER (TO MAKE THE
BEANSTALK GROW)

ONE 19-OUNCE CAN CANNELLINI
BEANS, UNDRAINED (THE MAGIC
BEANS)

ONE 13.75- TO 14.5-OUNCE CAN CHICKEN
BROTH (FOR EXTRA MEASURE)

1 CUP CARROT COINS (LIKE THE GOLD
COINS THE GIANT COUNTED)

1 STALK CELERY, SLICED (ABOUT
½ CUP) (LIKE A BEANSTALK)

½ TEASPOON GROUND CINNAMON (AS
IF JACK DIDN'T ALREADY HAVE
ENOUGH SPICE IN HIS LIFE)

1 TABLESPOON VEGETABLE OIL
(LIQUID GOLD)

1 WHOLE, SKINLESS, BONELESS
CHICKEN BREAST, CUT INTO 1-INCH
CUBES (HOPEFULLY NOT FROM THE
HEN THAT LAID THE GOLDEN EGGS)

1 CUP FROZEN GREEN BEANS (FROM
THE BEANSTALK)

1 CUP FINE EGG NOODLES (LIKE THE
STRINGS ON THE MAGIC HARP)

For the garnish:

½ CUP SLICED GREEN ONIONS (IN
CASE THE STORY MAKES YOU CRY)

1 CUP SHREDDED CHEDDAR CHEESE
(MADE FROM THE MILK OF THE
VERY COW JACK TRADED FOR THE
MAGIC BEANS)

Sharon Stine, Mary Lou Newhouse, and the fourth graders at the Central School in South Burlington, Vermont, developed this recipe for a hearty but simple chicken and vegetable soup. It satisfied the students' hunger for learning (by teaching them about fractions) as well as their hunger for soup. They donated their charity award to the Vermont Institute of Natural Science and the Friends of Music for Youth.

1. In a 5-quart Dutch oven, mix together the spaghetti sauce, water, cannellini beans, chicken broth, carrots, celery, and cinnamon. Bring to a boil over medium-high heat, turn the heat to low, cover, and simmer for 30 minutes.

2. While the soup is simmering, heat the vegetable oil in a 12-inch skillet over medium-high heat. Cook the chicken for 3–5 minutes, until tender and opaque.

3. Add the green beans and egg noodles to the Dutch oven. Bring to a boil over high heat. Turn the heat to low, cover the pot, and simmer for another 5 minutes, or until the noodles are cooked al dente, just barely tender. Stir in the chicken and heat through.

4. Serve in large soup bowls. Garnish with the green onions and cheese. Accompany the soup with sliced French bread (in place of the bread the giant wanted to make from Jack's bones).

SERVES 8

Stone Soup

In 1994, Karen Clement and her first graders at the Terra Linda School in Beaverton, Oregon, were inspired by the classic children's fairy tale Stone Soup *to create their own version. Their recipe, which includes Newman's Own Sockarooni Spaghetti Sauce, a stone, and a few plain, ordinary ingredients from the supermarket, magically turned into a winner for their favorite charity, their school.*

1. Place the stone in 2 cups of the water and boil it for 5 minutes to kill the germs. Throw away the water.

2. Put the stone, the remaining 8 cups of water, beef broth, salt, pepper, stew meat, and onion into an 8-quart soup pot. Simmer on low heat for about 2 hours. Skim occasionally with a spoon or ladle to remove the scum that rises to the top; continue skimming until no more scum appears.

3. Add the spaghetti sauce, carrots, celery, potatoes, and beans. Continue to simmer for 20 minutes, until the vegetables are tender. Add the pasta and cook for another 10–15 minutes, until the pasta is al dente (just barely tender).

4. Remove the stone before eating the soup, or you may hurt your teeth.

5. Serve the soup with warm bread and butter.

SERVES ONE CLASS OF 24 FIRST GRADERS OR 8 ADULTS

1 SMALL STONE
10 CUPS WATER (2 CUPS TO BOIL THE STONE, 8 CUPS FOR THE SOUP)
ONE 10½-OUNCE CAN BEEF BROTH
1 TEASPOON SALT
1 TEASPOON PEPPER
2 POUNDS BEEF STEW MEAT, CUT INTO 1-INCH CUBES
1 LARGE ONION, SLICED
ONE 26-OUNCE JAR NEWMAN'S OWN SOCKAROONI SPAGHETTI SAUCE, NEWMAN'S OWN BOMBOLINA SAUCE, OR YOUR FAVORITE MEATLESS SPAGHETTI SAUCE
4 CARROTS, SLICED
4 STALKS CELERY, SLICED
10 SMALL NEW POTATOES, CUT INTO CHUNKS
ONE 12-OUNCE PACKAGE ITALIAN GREEN BEANS, OR 8 OUNCES GREEN BEANS, BROKEN INTO 1-INCH PIECES
1 CUP UNCOOKED ABC PASTA

Camp is a place where you learn to live life better because you can do all sorts of things you thought you'd never do again, like fishing or horseback riding, because it's hard getting on a horse even without having had a stroke. Camp teaches you that you can do other things than lie in a hospital bed or lie in a grave forever. I think it's real cool that it doesn't cost anything because the kids don't have much money left because they paid all the hospital bills. And it's great that they can finally go have fun. And live while they can. I met new people, and it's so good to meet other sick kids because they can help you through when you're having trouble, and you help them when they're down. Like I helped David. He was really crying 'cause he had cancer in his brain, and I talked to him and I cheered him up. He was so cute, I just couldn't resist. I told him my story, that I had a brain tumor and I got radiation and now it's all gone. It made him feel better because I gave him hope that he'll be better. The best part of cheering somebody up is that you've got a good friend. And maybe when you're down, he'll cheer you up. I don't care if my boyfriend has no hair because I was like that, too. I'm not afraid to see it. I think that hope and love and laughing and confidence are all over camp; in a way they're growing as much as the grass is.

Katie,
camper

Julia Roberts's Baked Potato Soup

Julia Roberts acting in the 1997 gala

This rustic soup with crunchy potato skins and lots of chives has never failed. You will love it. To chop the chives, line them up evenly and cut them into very small segments with a knife or scissors.

1. Preheat the oven to 400°F.
2. Scrub the potatoes carefully with a brush to remove all dirt and pierce the skins in several places. Do not wrap them with foil; the skin should get crisp. Bake the potatoes for 1 hour, or until soft.
3. In a stockpot, heat the oil over medium-high heat. Add the garlic and onion, and sauté for a few minutes, until soft and translucent.
4. Peel 3 potatoes but leave the other 3 unpeeled. Cut all of them in half. Sauté for about 3 minutes in the hot oil.
5. Add the stock, plus water if necessary, so the liquid covers the vegetables by 2 inches. Bring the stock to a boil over high heat. Turn the heat to medium-low and cook, uncovered, for 35 minutes.
6. Puree the soup in a blender. Don't use a food processor; it makes the texture gummy. Add salt and pepper to taste, being careful not to overseason. Stir the finely chopped chives into the blended soup.
7. Place the soup in bowls and garnish each serving with a dollop of sour cream. Scatter the crumbled bacon on top and finish with a sprinkling of chopped chives.

SERVES 6

For the soup:
6 BOILING POTATOES (PREFERABLY WHITE ROSE)
¼ CUP MILD-FLAVORED COOKING OIL
3 CLOVES GARLIC, PEELED
1 ONION, CHOPPED
6 CUPS CHICKEN STOCK OR CANNED CHICKEN BROTH
SALT AND PEPPER
1 BUNCH CHIVES, CHOPPED AS FINELY AS POSSIBLE (ABOUT ¼ CUP)

For the garnish:
½ CUP SOUR CREAM
½ CUP CRUMBLED, COOKED BACON (ABOUT 8 SLICES)
1 BUNCH CHIVES, CHOPPED (ABOUT ¼ CUP)

Stomp "Jailhouse Rock" Beef Chili

The cast of Stomp
performing at the camp gala

For the chili:
2 POUNDS LEAN CHUCK MEAT
¼ CUP MILD-FLAVORED COOKING OIL
1 SMALL ONION, CHOPPED
8 CLOVES GARLIC, FINELY CHOPPED
½ CUP CHILI POWDER
1 QUART (4 CUPS) CHICKEN STOCK OR
    CANNED BROTH
2 TABLESPOONS GROUND CUMIN
¼ TEASPOON CAYENNE PEPPER
1 TABLESPOON BROWN SUGAR
½ CUP PEELED AND CHOPPED FRESH
    (PREFERABLY) OR CANNED
    TOMATOES
2 TEASPOONS SALT

For the thickening:
3 TABLESPOONS FLOUR
⅓ CUP WHITE OR YELLOW CORNMEAL
1 CUP WATER

This hearty chili calls for meat cubes, not ground meat, and plenty of garlic. If you (or your children) don't love garlic, decrease the amount. Serve with Sweet Corn Bread muffins (page 88) or garnish with crumbled soda crackers, or both.

1. Trim the meat of excess fat and cut it into ½-inch cubes. Pat it dry with paper towels.

2. In a large, heavy pot, heat the oil on high heat. When it is hot, add the meat cubes and sear until browned on all sides, about 5 minutes. Turn the heat to medium. Add the onion, garlic, and chili powder, and continue to cook for 10 minutes more, stirring the meat and vegetables so they do not burn. The vegetables should be soft, and the chili powder should turn a rich dark color.

3. Add the chicken stock. Cover the pot, turn the heat to medium-low, and simmer the chili for 1 hour, stirring occasionally.

4. Add the cumin, cayenne pepper, brown sugar, tomatoes, and salt. Simmer 15 minutes more, still covered and still stirring occasionally. If the chili starts sticking or gets too thick, add water.

5. Remove from the heat. Skim off any excess grease with a spoon.

6. Mix the flour, cornmeal, and water together and pour over the chili, stirring to mix well. Turn the heat to medium and cook 5 minutes more, stirring constantly to prevent sticking. Add more water if the chili is too thick. Taste for seasoning.

SERVES 4–6

Head 'Em Off at the Pass White Chili

You can make this lightning-fast chicken chili in about 20 minutes using canned and frozen products. It's also a great way to recycle yesterday's roast or stewed chicken. Janet Harrison English, food editor at The Clarion-Ledger *in Jackson, Mississippi, who came up with this easy recipe, donated her award to the Community Stew Pot Food Bank.*

1. In a 2-quart saucepan, sauté the onion in the oil until translucent.

2. Add the chopped chicken and mix thoroughly. Stir in the chicken broth, cannellini beans and their liquid, celery salt, oregano, and ½ cup of the salsa.

3. Simmer over medium heat for 10 minutes, stirring occasionally. Be careful not to break up the beans.

4. Just before serving, stir in 1 cup of the mozzarella cheese. Serve in individual bowls, garnished with the remaining mozzarella and salsa.

SERVES 4

½ CUP CHOPPED ONION (USE PRE-CHOPPED FROZEN ONIONS IF YOU'RE REALLY IN A RUSH)

1 TABLESPOON OLIVE OIL

1½ CUPS COOKED CHOPPED CHICKEN (OR TWO 5-OUNCE CANS CHICKEN)

½ CUP CHICKEN BROTH

TWO 15-OUNCE CANS CANNELLINI BEANS WITH THEIR LIQUID

½ TEASPOON CELERY SALT

1 TEASPOON OREGANO

ONE 11-OUNCE JAR NEWMAN'S OWN SALSA (MILD, MEDIUM, OR HOT) OR YOUR FAVORITE (½ CUP FOR THE CHILI, THE REST FOR THE GARNISH)

1½ CUPS SHREDDED MOZZARELLA CHEESE (1 CUP FOR THE CHILI, THE REST FOR THE GARNISH)

CHAPTER 2 — Sandwiches and Pizzas

Sausage Sandwiches

Grilled Chicken Burritos with Jack Cheese and Black Bean Salsa

Bagelroonies

Tic-Tac-Toe Quesadillas

Paul's Pocketful o' Peas

Vegetarian Sloppy Pauls

Talking Tortilla Hands

Eggstraordinary Egg Salad

The Lord's Dish . . . or Somebody Up There Likes Me Pizza

Cy Coleman's Barbecue Cheeseburger Pizza

Tony Randall's Sausage and Roasted Pepper Pizza

Strike Up the Band Pizza

Sausage Sandwiches

These are great additions to a picnic basket or lunch box. The smoked Gouda cheese tastes wonderful with the sausage. If it's too exotic for your children's taste, substitute sliced provolone or cheddar in their sandwiches and save the Gouda for your own.

1. Slice the sausages lengthwise but do not detach the 2 halves; flatten them out. In a large sauté pan, heat the oil over medium-high heat until hot. Cook the sausages on both sides. Remove from the heat and drain on paper towels.

2. Slice the sourdough rolls lengthwise but do not detach the 2 halves. Leave a sturdy "hinge" so the sandwiches will not come apart when you stuff them. Spread the butter on the cut surfaces. Reheat the sauté pan and brown the cut sides of the rolls until golden.

3. Spread 1 tablespoon of honey mustard on each roll. Top with 1 tablespoon of barbecue sauce, a sausage (opened flat), a slice of tomato, and a slice of cheese. Press the halves of the rolls closed.

SERVES 6

6 CHICKEN OR TURKEY SAUSAGES
1 TABLESPOON COOKING OIL
6 SOURDOUGH ROLLS, ABOUT
   6 INCHES LONG
3 TABLESPOONS BUTTER, SOFTENED
6 TABLESPOONS HONEY MUSTARD
6 TABLESPOONS BUTCH BARBECUE
   SAUCE (PAGE 57), OR YOUR
   FAVORITE
6 SLICES TOMATO
6 SLICES SMOKED GOUDA CHEESE

Grilled Chicken Burritos with Jack Cheese and Black Bean Salsa

For the burritos:

1 BONELESS CHICKEN BREAST HALF
(ABOUT 6 OUNCES)

⅓ CUP NEWMAN'S OWN BOMBOLINA
SAUCE OR YOUR FAVORITE MEAT-
LESS SPAGHETTI SAUCE

⅔ CUP BLACK BEANS, EITHER HOME-
COOKED OR CANNED AND DRAINED

4 TABLESPOONS NEWMAN'S OWN
MEDIUM SALSA OR YOUR FAVORITE

2 LARGE FLOUR TORTILLAS
(11–14 INCHES IN DIAMETER)

2 OUNCES MONTEREY JACK CHEESE,
GRATED

For the salad:

½ HEAD ROMAINE LETTUCE

2 TABLESPOONS NEWMAN'S OWN
CAESAR DRESSING OR YOUR
FAVORITE

Scott Cohen, former chef at the Stanhope Hotel on Fifth Avenue in New York, submitted this recipe. Chef Cohen has used his talents to benefit such charitable organizations as the League for the Hard of Hearing, Citymeals-on-Wheels, and SOS Taste of the Nation. For a simple but balanced meal, serve this tasty burrito with a romaine lettuce salad.

1. Preheat the oven to 400°F.

2. Put the chicken breast between 2 pieces of waxed paper. With a meat pounder or the rounded side of an empty bottle, pound the chicken until it is ¼ inch thick.

3. On any type of grill, stovetop or stand-alone, lightly grill the chicken on both sides until cooked through. Remove the cooked chicken and cut it into small strips.

4. In a small bowl, combine the spaghetti sauce with the chicken strips and set aside. In another small bowl, combine the black beans with the salsa and set aside.

5. Place half of the chicken mixture on 1 tortilla, spreading it evenly over the lower half and keeping the upper half empty. Top the chicken mixture with half of the black bean–salsa mixture and cheese. Roll up the burrito snugly around the filling. Repeat with the other tortilla.

6. Put the burritos on an ovenproof dish, seam side down, and bake until the cheese is melted inside, about 5 minutes. Remove to a serving plate.

7. TO MAKE THE SALAD: Discard the tough or wilted outer leaves of the romaine lettuce. Cut off the stem end and separate the head into leaves. Wash the leaves, pat dry with paper towels, and tear into bite-sized pieces. Toss the prepared lettuce with the salad dressing.

SERVES 2

Bagelroonies

Dana Reed, a teacher at West View Middle School in Morristown, Tennessee, used the Newman's Own recipe contest to teach basic English and math skills. She donated the award from these prize-winning Bagelroonies to the Special Olympics.

1. Preheat the broiler.
2. Cut the bagels in half. Spread each half with margarine.
3. Working in several batches, cook the Canadian bacon in a heavy skillet or the microwave until crisp. Drain on paper towels, cut into small pieces, and set aside.
4. Spoon the spaghetti sauce onto the bagel halves, approximately 3 tablespoons per half. Put the bacon pieces on top of the sauce, dividing it equally among the bagel halves.
5. Sprinkle each half with mozzarella and then Parmesan cheese.
6. Broil until the cheese melts.

SERVES 6

6 ONION BAGELS
6 TABLESPOONS SOFT-SPREAD
  MARGARINE
ONE 18-OUNCE PACKAGE SLICED
  CANADIAN BACON
ONE 14-OUNCE JAR NEWMAN'S OWN
  SOCKAROONI SPAGHETTI SAUCE OR
  YOUR FAVORITE MEATLESS
  SPAGHETTI SAUCE
ONE 16-OUNCE BAG SHREDDED
  MOZZARELLA CHEESE
FRESHLY GRATED PARMESAN CHEESE

ONE 12½-OUNCE CAN TUNA FISH,
  DRAINED
9–10 BLACK OLIVES (6 CHOPPED AND
  3–4, WITHOUT PITS, SLICED INTO 12
  CIRCLES, 3 OR 4 PER OLIVE)
1 MEDIUM GREEN ONION, SLICED
½ CUP SOUR CREAM, AT ROOM
  TEMPERATURE
8 FLOUR TORTILLAS
1 CUP WHOLE-KERNEL YELLOW CORN
1 POUND CHEDDAR CHEESE, GRATED
¾ CUP NEWMAN'S OWN MEDIUM
  SALSA OR YOUR FAVORITE
1⅓ CUPS GRATED MONTEREY JACK
  CHEESE
2 SMALL CANS MILD GREEN CHILES,
  CUT INTO THIN STRIPS

This playful interpretation of quesadillas, created by students from Centennial Middle School in Miami, Florida, is also delicious with diced chicken instead of the tuna fish, or with no meat for a purely vegetarian dish. The students donated their award to their school.

1. Preheat the oven to 350°F. Lightly coat 2 large baking sheets with nonstick cooking spray.

2. In a small bowl, combine the tuna fish, chopped olives, green onion, and sour cream. Set aside.

3. Place 2 tortillas on each baking sheet. Divide the tuna mixture evenly among the 4 tortillas, putting a dab in the center of each and spreading evenly out to the edges.

4. Layer each tortilla with ¼ cup of corn, ¼ of the grated cheddar cheese, and 3 tablespoons of salsa.

5. Place the remaining tortillas on top of the 4 on the baking sheets and sprinkle with Monterey Jack cheese. Arrange chile strips in a tic-tac-toe grid on each, and fill each grid with 3 olive circles.

6. Bake for approximately 15 minutes, until the cheese melts and the quesadillas are heated through. Cut into wedges.

SERVES 4–6

Dear Mr. Newman:

I am 13 years old, and I find that I really enjoy your Olive Oil and Vinegar Dressing. It doesn't make my mom have heartburn like other dressings we have tried, doesn't give me a stomachache, and doesn't give my father the squirts. My father, Ed, said that he finds he doesn't go to the bathroom as much as he did before. All this is true. You have to believe me, I'm not lying.

Sabrina

ONE 16-OUNCE PACKAGE FROZEN PEAS, THAWED

3 CUPS SHREDDED LETTUCE

2 CARROTS, GRATED

3 GREEN ONIONS, THINLY SLICED

1 MEDIUM RED PEPPER, DICED

1 MEDIUM GREEN PEPPER, DICED

ONE 8-OUNCE BOTTLE NEWMAN'S OWN RANCH DRESSING OR YOUR FAVORITE

6 SMALL PITAS, ABOUT 6 INCHES IN DIAMETER

1 CUP SHREDDED CHEDDAR CHEESE

laine Luschas and the summer campers at the Bloomsburg, Pennsylvania, YMCA created a prize-winning recipe by filling pitas (pocket bread) with a mixture of crisp and soft vegetables marinated in Newman's Own Ranch Dressing. The campers donated their award to the YMCA.

1. In a large mixing bowl, combine the peas, lettuce, carrots, onions, and peppers. Pour the salad dressing over the vegetables, mix thoroughly, and chill for 1 hour.

2. Cut the pita pockets in half crosswise and stuff each half first with the vegetable mixture and then with the cheese.

MAKES 12 PITA POCKETS

The dining hall at the camp

Vegetarian Sloppy Pauls

Three teenagers, Megan Kilpatrick, Trevyn Leighton, and Katharine Leighton, entered Newman's Own recipe contest to raise money for the Human Service Alliance in Winston-Salem, North Carolina. Their vegetarian update of the classic "sloppy joe" features salsa, vegetarian spaghetti sauce, and tofu. Serve it on whole wheat hamburger buns.

Health food stores and well-stocked supermarkets carry both tofu and whole wheat buns.

1. In a 12-inch skillet over medium heat, sauté the onion and peppers in 2 tablespoons of oil until tender.

2. Add the spaghetti sauce, salsa, chili powder, soy sauce, molasses, salt, and pepper. Simmer over low heat for 15 minutes.

3. While the sauce is simmering, brown the tofu in a 10-inch skillet over medium-high heat, using the remaining 2 tablespoons of oil. Add the Kitchen Bouquet.

4. When the tofu is well browned and the Kitchen Bouquet has been absorbed, add the contents of the skillet to the sauce. Mix thoroughly and simmer for 10 minutes.

SERVES 4–6

1 LARGE ONION, DICED
1½ MEDIUM GREEN PEPPERS, DICED
4 TABLESPOONS OLIVE OIL (HALF FOR SAUTÉING THE VEGETABLES, HALF FOR THE TOFU)
ONE 26-OUNCE JAR NEWMAN'S OWN SOCKAROONI SPAGHETTI SAUCE OR YOUR FAVORITE MEATLESS SPAGHETTI SAUCE
ONE 8-OUNCE JAR NEWMAN'S OWN MEDIUM SALSA OR YOUR FAVORITE
1½ TABLESPOONS CHILI POWDER
1 TABLESPOON SOY SAUCE
1 TABLESPOON MOLASSES
1 TEASPOON SALT
⅛ TEASPOON BLACK PEPPER
1½ POUNDS FIRM TOFU, DRAINED, PATTED DRY, AND CRUMBLED
1 TABLESPOON KITCHEN BOUQUET

NONSTICK COOKING SPRAY

16 FLOUR TORTILLAS (9–10 INCHES IN
   DIAMETER)

1 TABLESPOON CHILI POWDER

1 TABLESPOON SALT

TWO 11-OUNCE JARS NEWMAN'S OWN
   SALSA OR YOUR FAVORITE

BANDITO CHEESE OR SPINACH IN BAN-
   DITO DISGUISE (RECIPES FOLLOW)

When Barbara Juenker was teaching her first graders about people with special needs, she hit upon the idea of using cutout flour tortillas instead of cutout paper hands to teach the basics of sign language. She and her students at Mater Christi School in Burlington, Vermont, then created two dips for the "talking hands." After all, children's hands are usually busy dipping into something! The award for this creation was donated to the Special Olympics and Mater Christi School.

You will need a small hand-shaped cookie cutter or cardboard stencil. Baking supply stores and party stores frequently carry specialty cutters, or you can easily make a stencil by drawing a hand on a piece of cardboard and cutting it out.

You will also need a small shaker jar with small holes in the lid for sprinkling the seasoning on the "hands."

1. Preheat the oven to 350°F. Lightly coat 2 cookie sheets with nonstick cooking spray.

2. Cut the tortillas into hand shapes using the cutter or cut around the cardboard stencil with a knife. Depending on the size of your pattern, you should be able to get 2 or 3 "hands" from each tortilla.

3. In a small bowl, mix the chili powder and salt. Spoon the mixture into the shaker jar.

4. Place a tortilla cutout on a piece of waxed paper and coat lightly with cooking spray. Firmly press down the middle 2 fingers to form the sign language symbol for "I love you." Repeat with the other tortillas.

5. Lightly coat the tops of the bent fingers with cooking spray and sprinkle the seasoning mixture over the hands. Put the tortillas on the prepared cookie sheets. You may have to work in several batches.

6. Bake until lightly browned and crisp, about 8 minutes. Remove the tortillas from the pans and cool on wire racks.

7. Serve with the salsa, Bandito Cheese, or Spinach in Bandito Disguise.

MAKES 32–64 "HANDS"

TO MAKE BANDITO CHEESE: Heat the cheese and salsa together in a saucepan over medium heat, stirring occasionally, until the cheese is melted. Or microwave on high power for 5–7 minutes, stirring the mixture after about 3 minutes. Serve warm as a dip for the tortillas.

MAKES 5–6 CUPS

Bandito Cheese
1 POUND PASTEURIZED PROCESS
   CHEESE SPREAD
ONE 11-OUNCE JAR NEWMAN'S OWN
   SALSA OR YOUR FAVORITE

1. TO MAKE SPINACH IN BANDITO DISGUISE: Preheat the oven to 350°F. Lightly grease a 10-inch baking dish or quiche pan.

2. Squeeze the spinach dry, a handful at a time, using a clean dishtowel or paper towels.

3. Combine the salsa, cream cheese, and grated cheese in a medium bowl. Stir until well blended. Add the spinach and stir until evenly distributed.

4. Spoon the mixture into the prepared pan. Bake until melted and bubbly, about 25 minutes.

MAKES 5–6 CUPS

Spinach in Bandito Disguise
ONE 10-OUNCE PACKAGE FROZEN
   CHOPPED SPINACH, THAWED
ONE 11-OUNCE JAR NEWMAN'S OWN
   SALSA OR YOUR FAVORITE
ONE 8-OUNCE PACKAGE CREAM
   CHEESE, SOFTENED
1½ CUPS GRATED COLBY OR MON-
   TEREY JACK CHEESE

Eggstraordinary Egg Salad

6 EGGS
¼ CUP CHOPPED CELERY
¼ CUP LOW-FAT MAYONNAISE
2 TABLESPOONS DIJON MUSTARD
¼ CUP PICKLE RELISH
1½ TEASPOONS PAPRIKA
½ TEASPOON SALT
¼ TEASPOON LEMON PEPPER

metal frying basket, colander, or large flat sieve makes it easy to lower the eggs into the simmering water and to take them out all at once.

1. In a saucepan large enough to hold the eggs in 1 layer, bring enough water to a boil to cover them by 1 inch. Carefully lower the eggs into the water, turn down the heat, and gently boil for 14 minutes. Don't let the water boil so hard that the eggs bump together and crack.

2. As soon as the eggs are cooked, remove from the heat and plunge into a large bowl of cold water. This helps prevent an ugly gray ring from forming around the yolk. Peel the eggs when they are cool enough to handle.

3. In a medium bowl, chop the eggs coarsely, add the rest of the ingredients, and mash the mixture with a fork.

4. Unless you are using the salad immediately, cover with plastic wrap and refrigerate.

SERVES 6 AS SANDWICHES OR 4 AS A SALAD ON GREENS

The Lord's Dish . . . or Somebody Up There Likes Me Pizza

Julie Leberer and her students at the Mount St. Vincent Home for Children in Denver created an easy south-of-the-border pizza recipe using tortillas instead of traditional pizza dough. This recipe makes one tortilla-sized pizza; for more, just multiply everything times the number of eaters. The students donated their charity award to the Mount St. Vincent Home.

Served with an ice-cold glass of lemonade, either Newman's Own Old Fashioned Roadside Virgin Lemonade or your own favorite brand, this spicy pizza makes a great after-school snack.

1. Preheat the oven to 375°F.
2. Sprinkle the cheeses evenly on the tortilla. Smother with the spaghetti sauce. Arrange the pepperoni and jalapeño pepper on top.
3. Put the pizza on an ungreased cookie sheet and bake approximately 10 minutes, or until the cheeses are melted and bubbly.

SERVES 1

1 TABLESPOON SHREDDED MOZZARELLA CHEESE

1 TABLESPOON SHREDDED CHEDDAR CHEESE

1 FLOUR TORTILLA (6 INCHES IN DIAMETER)

2 TABLESPOONS NEWMAN'S OWN SOCKAROONI SPAGHETTI SAUCE OR YOUR FAVORITE MEATLESS SPAGHETTI SAUCE

6 SLICES PEPPERONI

1 TEASPOON DICED JALAPEÑO PEPPER OR CANNED MILD GREEN CHILES

Cy Coleman's Barbecue Cheeseburger Pizza

For the crust:

2 PREPARED PIZZA CRUSTS, 12–14
   INCHES IN DIAMETER, BAKED OR
   UNBAKED

For the topping:

1 TABLESPOON VEGETABLE OIL

8 OUNCES LEAN GROUND BEEF

1 SMALL ONION, THINLY SLICED OR
   FINELY CHOPPED

½ CUP BUTCH BARBECUE SAUCE (PAGE
   57) OR YOUR FAVORITE

¾ CUP SHREDDED MOZZARELLA
   CHEESE

¾ CUP FINELY CUBED MONTEREY JACK
   OR FONTINA CHEESE

SALT AND PEPPER TO TASTE

For an adult version of this kid-friendly pizza, substitute ½ cup of crumbled goat cheese for the Monterey Jack or fontina and lighten the toppings: Use only ½ cup of mozzarella and ¼ pound of ground beef for the 2 pizzas.

*P*repared pizza dough makes this recipe as easy as pie—pizza pie. For the dough, use whatever is available at your supermarket: frozen or raw pizza dough, or refrigerated packaged pizza dough (the kind in the cylindrical tin), or even completely baked, packaged pizza crust. Follow the manufacturer's directions for prebaking raw dough before adding the toppings.

For best results bake the pizzas one at a time. If you're in a hurry, however, you can bake both at once, positioning the trays one above the other in the middle of the racks and switching them from top to bottom partway through the baking.

1. Preheat the oven to 500°F. Lightly grease 2 pizza pans or cookie sheets.

2. Prepare and shape the pizza dough according to the manufacturer's instructions. If you are using raw dough, partially prebake the crusts by placing in the oven for 3–4 minutes, until pale brown and lightly crusted on top.

3. Heat the oil in a sauté pan over high heat. When it is hot, add the beef, brown it lightly, and remove it from the pan. In the same pan, sauté the onion for 5 minutes, until soft and translucent. Remove from the heat and set aside.

4. Brush each crust with half of the barbecue sauce. Sprinkle half of the onion, half of the ground beef, and half of the mozzarella cheese on each pizza. Dot evenly with the Monterey Jack cheese so that there will be cheese on every slice when the pizza is cut. If you wish, season with salt and pepper.

5. Bake for 6–12 minutes, checking frequently to make sure the crust does not burn. Remove from the oven and cool for 2 minutes. Cut with a pizza cutter.

SERVES 4–6

Tony Randall's Sausage and Roasted Pepper Pizza

Instead of using hamburger or pepperoni, this easy pizza uses low-fat chicken sausage. You can buy roasted peppers in glass jars at your supermarket. See the introduction to Cy Coleman's Barbecue Cheeseburger Pizza, page 36, for information on purchasing the pizza dough and for best baking results.

1. Preheat the oven to 500°F.

2. Prepare and shape the pizza dough according to the manufacturer's instructions. If you are using raw dough, partially prebake the crusts by placing in the oven for 3–4 minutes, until pale brown and lightly crusted on top.

3. Mix the olive oil with the salt, pepper, and curry powder. Set aside.

4. Slice the chicken sausages so that you have 1 piece for each slice of pizza.

5. Heat the cooking oil in a skillet on high heat and sauté the sausage slices for 3 minutes, or until golden brown. Set aside.

6. Using a pastry brush, spread 1 pizza crust with half of the olive oil mixture. Top with half of the sausage, being sure to put some on each piece of pizza. Top with half of the tomatoes, pepper strips, and cheese. Repeat for the other pizza.

7. Bake for 6–12 minutes, checking frequently to see that the crust does not burn. Remove and cool for 2 minutes. Cut into slices with a pizza cutter.

Serves 4–6

James Naughton and Tony Randall on stage at the camp

For the crust:

2 PREPARED PIZZA CRUSTS, 12–14 INCHES IN DIAMETER, BAKED OR UNBAKED

For the topping:

2 TABLESPOONS EXTRA-VIRGIN OLIVE OIL

¼ TEASPOON SALT

½ TEASPOON BLACK PEPPER

½ TEASPOON CURRY POWDER

2 LARGE CHICKEN OR TURKEY SAUSAGES

1 TEASPOON COOKING OIL

2 TOMATOES, FINELY CHOPPED

2 ROASTED PEPPERS, PATTED DRY AND SLICED INTO NARROW STRIPS

2 CUPS SHREDDED MOZZARELLA CHEESE

For the crust:
1 PREPARED PIZZA CRUST, 12–14
    INCHES IN DIAMETER, BAKED
    OR UNBAKED

For the topping:
3 BONELESS CHICKEN BREAST HALVES
1 CUP NEWMAN'S OWN LIGHT ITALIAN
    DRESSING OR YOUR FAVORITE
    (¾ CUP FOR THE MARINADE,
    ¼ CUP FOR THE TOPPING)
1 CUP NEWMAN'S OWN MARINARA
    STYLE VENETIAN SPAGHETTI SAUCE
    WITH MUSHROOMS OR YOUR
    FAVORITE
½ GREEN PEPPER, RIBS AND SEEDS
    REMOVED, SLICED INTO THIN
    STRIPS (ABOUT ½ CUP)
½ RED PEPPER, RIBS AND SEEDS
    REMOVED, SLICED INTO THIN
    STRIPS (ABOUT ½ CUP)
1½ CUPS GRATED PROVOLONE CHEESE
2 LARGE TOMATOES, THINLY SLICED
½ CUP GRATED PARMESAN CHEESE

Band members from Richard Montgomery High School in Rockville, Maryland, received a standing ovation for composing this pizza recipe. They donated their award to the band. If you don't have a barbecue grill, cook the chicken in the broiler. See the introduction to Cy Coleman's Barbecue Cheeseburger Pizza, page 36, for information on purchasing the pizza dough.

1. Lightly grease a cookie sheet.
2. Pierce the chicken breasts a couple of times with a fork. Marinate them for 1–2 hours in ¾ cup of the Italian dressing.
3. About 20 minutes before you plan to cook the chicken, preheat the barbecue grill or set the oven to broil.
4. Put the pizza crust on the prepared cookie sheet. Brush the crust lightly with the remaining ¼ cup of Italian dressing and prick with a fork. If the crust is unbaked, broil for 2 minutes, or until lightly browned, watching carefully so that it doesn't burn. Remove from the oven.
5. If you are using a barbecue grill for the chicken, lower the oven temperature to 350°F. If you are going to broil the chicken in the oven, leave the oven on broil. Remove the chicken from the marinade and grill or broil until cooked through.
6. Cut the chicken into strips. If you have not already done so, turn the oven to 350°F.
7. Spread the marinara sauce on the pizza crust. Layer the chicken, peppers, provolone cheese, tomatoes, and Parmesan cheese over the sauce. Bake the pizza until the cheese melts.

SERVES 2–3

CHAPTER 8 Main Courses

David Letterman's Baked Chicken in A+ Sauce

Harry Belafonte's Sloppy Joe Shortcakes

Lemonade Chicken Wings

Joan Rivers's Bombolina Baked Chicken over Rigatoni

Easy Kid Kabobs

Nathan Lane's Turkey Meatballs and Spaghetti

Perfect Pasta for Peace

Jerry Stiller's Roasted Turkey Breast

Triple-Threat Meat Loaf

Charlotte's Hole in the Wall Gang Camp Chop Suey

Amish Haystack Dinners

Fun and Games Fondue

Baked Hamburger Pasta Casserole

Baby Back Pork Ribs with Butch Barbecue Sauce

Pork and Beans

Penne with Tomato Salsa Sauce

Charlotte's Hole in the Wall Gang Camp Stuffed Shells

Tim Robbins's Crunchy Oven-Fried Snapper Fillets

Southern-Style Orange Roughy Fillets

Candice Bergen's Baked Halibut Fillets with Lemon, Peanuts, and Honey Mustard

Sarah Jessica Parker's Deviled Shrimp Salad

James Naughton's Creamy Baked Pasta

Layered Cheese Soufflé

To Whom It May Concern:

Enclosed please find our entry for the Newman's Own School-children's Recipe Contest.

My daughter's name is Allison, and she is 4½ years old. The preschool that she attends made a book of recipes for the mothers for Mother's Day. The teacher asked the children what their favorite dinner is and then asked the children to describe how they would cook that dinner. Here is my daughter's response and entry for the contest:

Pork Chops with Rice and Carrots

First you go shopping and get chicken and some carrots. Put them on the stove and then wait for them to cool. Get the chicken. You put it on the stove and then it turns to pork chops. Cook for just 1 minute. Pour in some Paul Newman. Then my mommy bakes them for 2 minutes, and then we put it on the table and we eat it.

Allison

David Letterman's Baked Chicken in A+ Sauce

This chicken soaks up the flavors of a spicy barbecue-based sauce, enhanced with balsamic vinegar. The sauce has a nice peppery bite; you can decrease the pepper if you like your barbecue mild, or increase it, up to four tablespoons, if you love "hot stuff." The extra sauce will keep well for about a month in the refrigerator, or it can be frozen.

1. To make the sauce, combine all the ingredients in a large bowl and stir well. Reserve 2 cups for the marinade and store the rest in a covered container in the refrigerator.

2. Put the chicken breasts in a shallow ovenproof dish large enough to hold the chicken in a single layer. Season lightly with salt and pepper, and pour the 2 reserved cups of sauce over them. Cover the dish with foil and place in the refrigerator for 1 hour to marinate the chicken.

3. About 20 minutes before you plan to cook the chicken, preheat the oven to 400°F.

4. Put the baking dish, marinade and all, in the oven and bake for 20 minutes. Turn over the breasts and bake another 15–20 minutes, or until the chicken is fully cooked.

SERVES 6

For the sauce (about 8 cups):
4 CUPS BUTCH BARBECUE SAUCE
   (PAGE 57) OR YOUR FAVORITE
1 CUP BALSAMIC VINEGAR
1¼ CUPS WORCESTERSHIRE SAUCE
¾ CUP DIJON MUSTARD
½ TEASPOON SALT
1 TABLESPOON BLACK PEPPER
¾ CUP CANOLA OR OTHER MILD-
   FLAVORED VEGETABLE OIL
¾ CUP OLIVE OIL

For the chicken:
6 CHICKEN BREAST HALVES (BONES IN
   AND SKIN ON)
SALT AND PEPPER TO TASTE

Harry Belafonte's Sloppy Joe Shortcakes

For the sloppy joes:
2 TABLESPOONS COOKING OIL
1 POUND GROUND DARK MEAT
    CHICKEN OR TURKEY
1 CUP CHOPPED YELLOW ONIONS
1 CUP CHOPPED CELERY
1 CUP CHOPPED TOMATOES, FRESH OR
    CANNED
ONE 24-OUNCE CAN TOMATO PUREE
¾ TEASPOON SALT
1 TEASPOON BLACK PEPPER
½ TEASPOON PAPRIKA

For the drop biscuits:
2 CUPS SIFTED ALL-PURPOSE FLOUR
3 TABLESPOONS BAKING POWDER
1 TEASPOON SALT
⅓ CUP CRISCO OR OTHER SOLID
    VEGETABLE SHORTENING
⅔ CUP WHOLE MILK
4 TEASPOONS UNSALTED BUTTER

These chicken or turkey sloppy joes, served over warm buttered drop biscuits, are much better than the standard variety made with ground beef and store-bought hamburger buns!

1. TO MAKE THE SLOPPY JOES: In a large cast-iron skillet, heat the oil on high until hot. Add the chicken and cook for 2 minutes.

2. Turn the heat to medium. Add the onions, celery, and tomatoes, and sauté, stirring to prevent sticking, until the chicken is golden brown, about 15 minutes.

3. Add the tomato puree, salt, pepper, and paprika. Stir to mix well.

4. Turn the heat to medium-low, cover, and simmer for 30 minutes. Remove the cover and continue simmering another 30 minutes, adding water if the mixture becomes too dry.

5. Preheat the oven to 450°F. Lightly grease a baking sheet.

6. TO MAKE THE BISCUITS: Combine the flour, baking powder, and salt in a medium bowl.

7. Add the vegetable shortening and milk at the same time. Stir with a fork until the mixture makes a ball in the bowl. Stop stirring as soon as the dough holds together. If you overmix the dough, the biscuits will be tough instead of light and flaky.

8. Drop the dough onto the baking sheet by rounded tablespoonfuls, keeping the mounds of dough about 1 inch apart. Bake for 10–15 minutes, or until the tops are lightly golden.

9. Remove from the baking sheet and cool briefly. While the biscuits are still warm, cut them in half and spread with the butter.

SERVES 3–4

Harry Belafonte and Whoopi Goldberg
performing at the 1996 camp gala

2 TABLESPOONS OLIVE OIL
2 TABLESPOONS BUTTER
2 SHALLOTS OR ½ MEDIUM ONION,
    FINELY CHOPPED (2 TABLESPOONS)
2 TEASPOONS DRIED ROSEMARY
½ CUP NEWMAN'S OWN OLD
    FASHIONED ROADSIDE VIRGIN
    LEMONADE OR YOUR FAVORITE
1 TEASPOON BLACK PEPPER
1 TEASPOON SALT
10–12 CHICKEN WINGS

emonade provides the zing in the sauce for these chicken wings. Serve them warm with rice as a meal, or at room temperature as a snack.

1. Preheat the oven to 425°F.

2. TO MAKE THE SAUCE: In a small saucepan, heat the oil and butter over medium heat until the butter is melted. Add the shallots and rosemary, and cook for 2–3 minutes.

3. Add the lemonade, pepper, and salt. Simmer over low heat for 6–8 minutes, until slightly reduced and syrupy. Set aside to cool.

4. TO COOK THE CHICKEN: Cut each chicken wing into 3 parts. Cut the wings apart at the joints with heavy-duty kitchen scissors or use a sharp knife with a stiff blade, inserting the blade between the bones to cut the joint apart. Throw away the wing tips, which don't have much meat on them.

5. Place the wing pieces in a shallow ovenproof pan or dish and coat well with the sauce.

6. Bake until the skin is golden brown, about 30 minutes.

MAKES 20–24 PIECES

Joan Rivers's Bombolina Baked Chicken over Rigatoni

Serve this easy oven-baked dish with a green salad and a loaf of Italian bread. You can use low-fat mozzarella cheese if you wish.

1. Preheat the oven to 350°F. Butter a 13 × 9-inch ovenproof dish.

2. Bring a large pot of salted water to a boil over high heat. Add the pasta, and quickly bring the water back to a boil. Stir the pasta a few times so it does not stick or clump together. Boil according to the manufacturer's directions but begin tasting the pasta several minutes before the suggested cooking time has elapsed. It should be tender but offer just a little resistance to your teeth.

3. Drain the pasta in a colander. Toss it in a bowl with the tomatoes, mushrooms, garlic, parsley, salt, and pepper. Add 1½ cups of the mozzarella cheese. Place in the prepared baking dish and set aside.

4. Heat the oil over high heat in a skillet large enough to hold the chicken in one layer. Brown the breasts on both sides in the hot oil.

5. Place the chicken breasts on top of the rigatoni in the baking dish. Pour the spaghetti sauce over the breasts and dot with the butter. Top with the remaining ½ cup of mozzarella cheese. Cover the baking dish with foil and bake for 35 minutes.

6. To serve, place a portion of the pasta on each plate. Put a chicken breast on top and scoop some of the spaghetti sauce on top of it. Sprinkle with the Parmesan cheese.

SERVES 6

1 POUND RIGATONI PASTA
3 CUPS PEELED AND DICED FRESH
   TOMATOES
1 CUP SLICED MUSHROOMS
2 TEASPOONS CHOPPED GARLIC
¼ CUP CHOPPED PARSLEY
SALT AND PEPPER TO TASTE
2 CUPS SHREDDED MOZZARELLA
   CHEESE (1½ CUPS FOR THE PASTA,
   ½ CUP FOR THE CHICKEN)
1 TABLESPOON COOKING OIL
6 BONELESS CHICKEN BREAST HALVES
2 CUPS NEWMAN'S OWN BOMBOLINA
   SAUCE OR YOUR FAVORITE MEAT-
   LESS SPAGHETTI SAUCE
6 TABLESPOONS BUTTER
½ CUP GRATED PARMESAN CHEESE
   FOR GARNISH

Easy Kid Kabobs

1 PINT (2 CUPS) CHERRY TOMATOES
1 RED ONION
1 GREEN PEPPER
1 PINT (2 CUPS) MUSHROOMS
2 WHOLE, BONELESS, SKINLESS
    CHICKEN BREASTS, CUT INTO
    "NUGGETS"
ONE 16-OUNCE BOTTLE NEWMAN'S
    OWN LIGHT ITALIAN DRESSING OR
    YOUR FAVORITE

Debbie Fullerton's class at Cesar Chavez School in Indio, California, won a prize with this healthy recipe for chicken and vegetable kabobs, marinated in Newman's Own Light Italian Dressing to add zip and zest. The fourth graders donated their charity award to the Children's Museum of the Desert.

Since the chicken and vegetables marinate overnight, you must start this dish the day before you plan to eat it.

1. Wash and dice the tomatoes, onion, pepper, and mushrooms.

2. Place the diced vegetables and chicken in a medium bowl. Pour the Italian dressing over them and mix well. Cover and refrigerate overnight.

3. Preheat the oven to 350°F.

4. Arrange the chicken and vegetables on skewers. Place in a baking dish and bake for 30–40 minutes, rotating the skewers after 15–20 minutes.

SERVES 4–6

Nathan Lane's Turkey Meatballs and Spaghetti

This recipe contains seasonings that are probably already in your spice rack or your kitchen cupboard. It's easy to prepare and has a hearty, homey flavor.

1. Preheat the oven to 400°F.
2. In a medium bowl, mix all the ingredients together except the spaghetti sauce. Form into 12 meatballs about 1½ inches in diameter.
3. Put the meatballs in a 9 × 5-inch baking dish, packing them in close together. Pour the spaghetti sauce over them and bake, uncovered, for 35–40 minutes.
4. While the meatballs are cooking, bring a large pot of salted water to a boil. After the meatballs have been cooking about 20 minutes, put the spaghetti in the pot and quickly bring the water back to a boil. Stir the pasta a few times so that it does not stick or clump together. Boil according to the manufacturer's directions but begin tasting the pasta several minutes before the suggested cooking time has elapsed. It should be tender but offer just a little resistance to your teeth. Drain the pasta in a colander but don't rinse it. Drizzle the oil over it to keep it from sticking while you finish the dish.
5. Heat the spaghetti sauce in a large pot.
6. When the meatballs are done, carefully spoon them out of their sauce and set aside. Scrape the sauce remaining in the baking dish into the pot of sauce. Put the cooked spaghetti into the pot and toss well to coat with the hot sauce.
7. To serve, place a portion of the sauced spaghetti in each of 4 large individual pasta bowls. Put 3 meatballs on top of each serving and sprinkle with the cheese.

Julia Roberts, Nathan Lane, and Paul Newman in a camp gala skit

For the meatballs:
1 POUND GROUND TURKEY
1 EGG
½ CUP SEASONED BREAD CRUMBS
1 TABLESPOON DRIED PARSLEY
1 CARROT, FINELY SHREDDED
  (ABOUT ½ CUP)
½ TEASPOON SALT
¾ TEASPOON BLACK PEPPER
1 TEASPOON GARLIC POWDER
1 TABLESPOON DRIED ONION
1 TABLESPOON WORCESTERSHIRE
  SAUCE
1 TEASPOON KETCHUP
JUICE OF 1 LEMON
1½ CUPS NEWMAN'S OWN MARINARA
  STYLE VENETIAN SPAGHETTI SAUCE
  OR YOUR FAVORITE

For the spaghetti:
1 POUND SPAGHETTI
1 TABLESPOON OLIVE OIL
1½ CUPS NEWMAN'S OWN MARINARA
  STYLE VENETIAN SPAGHETTI SAUCE
  OR YOUR FAVORITE
½ CUP GRATED PARMESAN CHEESE
  FOR GARNISH

SERVES 4

1 POUND FUSILLI PASTA OR YOUR
   FAVORITE SHORT, COMPACT SHAPE

1 SMALL CAULIFLOWER

1 HEAD BROCCOLI

1 MEDIUM ZUCCHINI

3 TABLESPOONS OLIVE OIL

3 CLOVES GARLIC, MINCED

1 SMALL RED ONION, FINELY CHOPPED

1 POUND TURKEY SAUSAGE, CUT INTO
   CHUNKS

8 FRESH BASIL LEAVES, CHOPPED

½ TABLESPOON DILL WEED

SALT AND FRESHLY GROUND PEPPER
   TO TASTE

ONE 10-OUNCE PACKAGE FROZEN CORN

3 CARROTS, SHREDDED

ONE 5-OUNCE JAR SPANISH OLIVES,
   DRAINED

ONE 26-OUNCE JAR NEWMAN'S OWN
   MARINARA STYLE VENETIAN
   SPAGHETTI SAUCE OR YOUR
   FAVORITE

CROUTONS FOR GARNISH

GRATED PARMESAN CHEESE FOR
   GARNISH

Fifteen second grade boys at the Allen-Stevenson School in New York City created this nutritious recipe that even a picky eater can enjoy. The second graders agreed that not everyone would like every ingredient, so they made up a list from which people could pick and choose, either before making the recipe or by "picking out" things on their plate. The boys donated their charity award to their school.

This recipe has many steps because all the different vegetables must be cut into bite-sized pieces, but it is not difficult. If your own personal Perfect Pasta includes only a few items from the list, it will require less cutting and chopping.

1. TO COOK THE PASTA: Bring a large pot of salted water to a boil over high heat. Add the pasta and quickly bring the water back to a boil. Stir the pasta a few times so it does not stick or clump together. Boil according to the manufacturer's directions but begin tasting the pasta several minutes before the suggested cooking time has elapsed. It should be tender but offer just a little resistance to your teeth.

2. Drain the pasta in a colander and run cold water over it to stop the cooking. Place in a bowl, cover and set aside.

3. TO PREPARE THE VEGETABLES: Remove the outer leaves from the cauliflower. Cut the head into quarters, remove and discard the central core, and cut the florets into bite-sized pieces.

4. Cut off and discard the tough lower ends of the broccoli stalks; trim the individual florets into bite-sized pieces. Peel off the tough skin covering the main stalks and slice the stalks into bite-sized pieces.

5. Scrub the zucchini carefully under running water until no dirt remains on the skin. Cut it crosswise into ¼-inch slices.

6. To make the sauce: In a large, heavy pot, heat the oil over medium heat. Add the garlic and onion, and sauté until soft but not brown. Add the turkey sausage and cook, covered, for approximately 10 minutes, until browned.

7. Add the cauliflower, broccoli, zucchini, basil, and dill. Season with salt and pepper. Simmer about 8–10 minutes, until the vegetables are fork-tender.

8. Add the corn, carrots, olives, and marinara sauce. Mix well and continue cooking over medium heat until heated through, stirring occasionally.

9. Add the cooked pasta to the vegetable-sausage mixture and stir well.

10. Serve topped with croutons and cheese.

SERVES 12 CHILDREN OR 8 ADULTS

Jerry Stiller's Roasted Turkey Breast

½ BONELESS TURKEY BREAST
  (2–4 POUNDS)
2–3 TABLESPOONS BUTTER, SOFTENED
½ CUP DIJON MUSTARD
½ CUP SOUR CREAM
1 TEASPOON SALT
1 TEASPOON BLACK PEPPER

This roasted turkey breast makes great sandwiches. Cook it the night before and slice it in the morning. Anything left over can be frozen, even in sliced portions.

1. Rinse the turkey breast with cold water and pat dry with paper towels. Rub the butter on the skin side of the breast.

2. Place the turkey breast, skin side down, in a shallow ovenproof dish. Combine the mustard, sour cream, salt, and pepper. Rub the marinade on the nonskin side of the turkey breast. Cover with foil and place in the refrigerator for 1 hour to marinate.

3. Preheat the oven to 400°F.

4. Roast the turkey breast, still skin side down, about 20 minutes per pound. The turkey is done when an instant-read thermometer inserted in the thickest part of the breast reads 160°F. Remove from the oven and let stand at least 20 minutes before carving.

SERVES 4–5 AS A MEAL OR MAKES ABOUT 12 SANDWICHES

Triple-Threat Meat Loaf

Meat Loaf and Hole in the Wall Gang Camp kids

Spice up this meat loaf with a dollop of Butch Barbecue Sauce (page 57) or your favorite bottled brand, and serve it with mashed potatoes and buttery corn. If you don't have an instant-read thermometer, you can test doneness by inserting a knife in the center of the meat loaf, waiting about thirty seconds, and removing it. The knife should come out steaming and be too hot to press against your lower lip.

Mix the meat with your clean hands, but be sure to wash them immediately afterwards.

Unless you bought the ground meat from a butcher, you probably had to buy more than the specified amounts. Just use the extra to make a second meat loaf and serve it in sandwiches. It also freezes well.

1. Preheat the oven to 375°F. Lightly grease a 9 × 5-inch loaf pan with cooking oil.

2. In a large bowl, mix all the ingredients together gently with your hands. Do not overwork the meat, or the meat loaf will lose its tender texture.

3. Pack the meat mixture into the loaf pan, mounding up the top. Make an indentation down the center and pour in just enough ketchup to fill it.

4. Bake for 45–55 minutes. The meat loaf is done when it feels firm and has shrunk away from the sides of the pan or when an instant-read thermometer inserted in the middle of the loaf reads 160°F. Remove from the oven and pour off the excess fat.

5. Cool the meat loaf for 10 minutes before slicing. You can invert the meat loaf on a serving platter and slice it at the table.

SERVES 6, WITH LEFTOVERS

8 OUNCES GROUND PORK
12 OUNCES LEAN GROUND BEEF
8 OUNCES GROUND CHICKEN OR TURKEY
2 EGGS
⅔ CUP SEASONED BREAD CRUMBS
¼ CUP WORCESTERSHIRE SAUCE
⅓ CUP DIJON MUSTARD
1 TEASPOON SALT
1 TEASPOON BLACK PEPPER
JUICE OF 1 LEMON
2 TABLESPOONS KETCHUP, PLUS EXTRA FOR THE TOP OF THE MEAT LOAF
¼ CUP CHOPPED ONION
1 TABLESPOON CHOPPED FRESH GARLIC
1 TABLESPOON BALSAMIC VINEGAR

Newman and campers John Faria, Josh Strout, Sarah Laaff, and Scott Duffy

8 OUNCES ELBOW MACARONI
1 TABLESPOON COOKING OIL
1 POUND GROUND BEEF
1 MEDIUM ONION, CHOPPED (ABOUT
    1 CUP)
4 LARGE SWEET PEPPERS, ANY COLOR,
    DICED
1 CLOVE GARLIC, MINCED
SALT AND PEPPER TO TASTE
1 CUP NEWMAN'S OWN MARINARA
    STYLE VENETIAN SPAGHETTI SAUCE
    OR YOUR FAVORITE
2 MEDIUM TOMATOES OR ONE
    1-POUND CAN PLUM TOMATOES,
    COARSELY CHOPPED

Charlotte's Hole in the Wall Gang Camp Chop Suey

*C*harlotte Werner is in charge of the kitchen at the camp. This and her recipe for stuffed shells (see page 60) are among the children's favorites. Serve it with garlic bread and a big salad (tossed with one of Newman's Own salad dressings).

1. Bring a large pot of salted water to a boil over high heat. Add the pasta and quickly bring the water back to a boil. Stir the pasta a few times so it does not stick or clump together. Boil according to the manufacturer's directions but begin tasting the pasta several minutes before the suggested cooking time has elapsed. It should be tender but offer just a little resistance to your teeth. Drain in a colander.

2. While the pasta is cooking, heat the oil in a heavy skillet over medium-high heat. Add the ground beef and cook, stirring constantly to break it up into small pieces.

3. Stir in the onion, peppers, garlic, salt, and pepper. Cook until all the vegetables are soft.

4. Add the marinara sauce and the tomatoes and stir gently. Cook until the tomatoes are heated through.

5. Place the cooked pasta in a large bowl. Add the ground beef mixture and gently stir to blend the ingredients.

SERVES 4–6

Amish Haystack Dinners

School nurse June Yoder, second grade teacher Judy Keil, and her students at the Honeyville School in Goshen, Indiana, won a grand prize with this recipe that reflects the children's Amish heritage. At an Amish haystack dinner, traditionally used as a way to raise money for the needy, guests build "haystacks" of lettuce, meat, cracker crumbs, and other ingredients. The students donated their charity award to help a local family devastated by a fire.

This is a great idea for a children's party meal, since it easily feeds twelve people and is fun to put together. For a moister "haystack," substitute 1½ cups of heated pasteurized processed cheese sauce for the grated cheddar cheese.

1. In a 12-inch skillet over medium-high heat, brown the ground beef with the taco seasoning. Add the spaghetti sauce and simmer until the meat is cooked through and the liquid evaporates.

2. Mix the crushed soda crackers and tortilla chips in a bowl.

3. Place the ground beef mixture, rice, and remaining ingredients in individual bowls.

4. Let your guests serve themselves. The traditional order for layering a "haystack" is lettuce, crushed crackers and chips, meat mixture, rice, tomatoes, carrots, onions, olives, pepper, celery, cheese, bacon, sunflower seeds, and salsa.

Serves 12

2 POUNDS LEAN GROUND BEEF

1 PACKAGE DRY TACO SEASONING MIX

ONE 14-OUNCE JAR (OR 1½ CUPS) NEWMAN'S OWN SOCKAROONI SPAGHETTI SAUCE OR YOUR FAVORITE MEATLESS SPAGHETTI SAUCE

2 CUPS CRUSHED SODA CRACKERS OR SALTINES

ONE 9-OUNCE BAG TORTILLA CHIPS, CRUSHED

2 CUPS COOKED RICE

1 HEAD ICEBERG LETTUCE, SHREDDED

2 CUPS DICED TOMATOES

1 CUP CHOPPED CARROTS

1 CUP CHOPPED ONIONS

1 CUP SLICED, PITTED RIPE OLIVES

1 CUP DICED GREEN PEPPER

1 CUP DICED CELERY

1½ CUPS SHREDDED CHEDDAR CHEESE

1 CUP CRUMBLED COOKED BACON

1 CUP SUNFLOWER SEEDS

ONE 11-OUNCE JAR NEWMAN'S OWN SALSA OR YOUR FAVORITE

I've never told anybody about what I have, because they always have one of two reactions. Either they feel sorry for me and treat me different, or they are afraid of catching it and run away. And I don't want to hear either of those.

But here, they all know what we have, but they don't treat us any different. They just take a little bit more care of us, so we can just go out and have fun. That's what's so great about this place. And that's why it's the best thing I've ever done.

— a camper

Fun and Games Fondue

Lois McAtee and her students from San Luis Rey School in Oceanside, California, scored high marks for this simple-to-make, fun-to-eat fondue. The children donated their charity award to the Multiple Sclerosis Society and their school. The fondue is also excellent served over warm pasta or rice.

1. In a 3-quart saucepan over high heat, cook the ground beef and onion until the meat is well browned. Spoon off any extra fat.

2. Stir in the spaghetti sauce and fennel seeds, and heat the fondue until it boils. Turn the heat to low and stir in the processed cheese and mozzarella. As soon as the cheese melts, remove the saucepan from the heat and pour the mixture into a fondue pot or warm bowl.

3. To serve, place the fondue pot on a large tray to catch the drips. Arrange the bread cubes, tortilla chips, and celery sticks on the same tray. Serve with colored cocktail toothpicks, fondue forks, or regular forks.

SERVES 6 AS A MAIN DISH OR 12 AS A SNACK

8 OUNCES LEAN GROUND BEEF
1 MEDIUM ONION, FINELY CHOPPED
ONE 26-OUNCE JAR NEWMAN'S OWN SOCKAROONI SPAGHETTI SAUCE OR YOUR FAVORITE MEATLESS SPAGHETTI SAUCE
¾ TEASPOON FENNEL SEEDS
1 CUP SHREDDED PASTEURIZED PROCESSED CHEESE FOOD
1 CUP SHREDDED MOZZARELLA CHEESE
CUBES OF FRENCH BREAD, TORTILLA CHIPS, AND CELERY STICKS FOR DIPPING

4 CUPS NEWMAN'S OWN SOCKAROONI
SPAGHETTI SAUCE OR YOUR
FAVORITE MEATLESS SPAGHETTI
SAUCE (¼ CUP FOR THE BURGERS,
THE REST FOR THE SAUCE)
1 TEASPOON SALT
½ TEASPOON PEPPER
2 POUNDS LEAN GROUND BEEF
1 BUNCH BROCCOLI, TRIMMED AND
CUT INTO FLORETS
1 POUND ROTELLE, FUSILLI, OR OTHER
SPIRAL-SHAPED PASTA
⅓ CUP GRATED PARMESAN CHEESE

ven picky eaters won't pick out the "green stuff" in this casserole. For instructions on improvising a steamer see page 80.

1. Preheat the oven to 375°F.

2. In a medium bowl, combine ¼ cup of the spaghetti sauce, salt, pepper, and meat. Mix lightly to blend well. Shape into 8 patties.

3. In a large skillet over medium heat, sauté the meat patties in their own fat until they are the way you like them. For medium burgers, cook approximately 4 minutes on each side.

4. Steam the broccoli in a steaming basket over 1 or 2 inches of boiling water until fork-tender, 3–4 minutes. Or boil, uncovered, in a large quantity of salted boiling water until just tender but still crisp, about 4 minutes.

5. Bring a large pot of salted water to a boil over high heat. Add the pasta and quickly bring the water back to a boil. Stir the pasta a few times so it does not stick or clump together. Boil according to the manufacturer's directions but begin tasting the pasta several minutes before the suggested cooking time has elapsed. It should be tender but offer just a little resistance to your teeth.

6. Drain the pasta in a colander and run cold water over it to stop the cooking.

7. Heat the remaining 3¾ cups of spaghetti sauce in a medium saucepan until just bubbling.

8. Arrange the burgers, broccoli, and pasta in alternating layers in a 3-quart casserole. Spoon the sauce over all. Sprinkle with the cheese. Bake until hot and bubbling, 15–20 minutes.

SERVES 8

Baby Back Pork Ribs with Butch Barbecue Sauce

You can make these ribs with commercially bottled dressing, but they will be even better with homemade Butch Barbecue Sauce. The homemade sauce keeps several weeks in the refrigerator or can be frozen. Plan on about one pound of ribs per adult.

This recipe has lots of ingredients, but it is not difficult. Most of the ingredients can simply be taken off the shelf and thrown into the pot.

1. To MAKE THE BARBECUE SAUCE: Heat the oil in a heavy 4-quart saucepan over high heat. Add the chopped garlic, onion, and horseradish, and cook for 1 minute.

2. Add all the other ingredients and bring to a boil. Turn the heat to medium and cook, uncovered, about 20 minutes, stirring frequently. Cool and remove the bay leaf.

3. To COOK THE PORK: Bring a large pot of water to a boil. Add the pork ribs, turn the heat to medium-low, and simmer until the meat almost falls off the bones, about 1 hour. Remove from the pot and let cool.

4. Preheat the oven to 400°F.

5. Cut each rack of ribs in half. Brush the ribs with about 1½ cups of the barbecue sauce. Reserve another 1½ cups for dipping.

6. Put the ribs in a baking dish and cover with foil. Bake the ribs for 20–25 minutes.

SERVES 6

For the Butch Barbecue Sauce (about 5 cups):

½ CUP CANOLA OR OTHER MILD-FLAVORED VEGETABLE OIL
¼ CUP CHOPPED GARLIC
¾ CUP CHOPPED YELLOW ONION
½ CUP PREPARED HORSERADISH
4 CUPS TOMATO PUREE
1 CUP DARK BROWN SUGAR
2½ CUPS WATER
¾ CUP CLOVER HONEY OR ANY MILD-FLAVORED HONEY
¼ CUP DARK MOLASSES
½ CUP TOMATO PASTE
½ CUP BALSAMIC VINEGAR
1 CUP WORCESTERSHIRE SAUCE
½ CUP DIJON MUSTARD
¼ CUP DRIED ONION
¼ CUP GRANULATED GARLIC
1 TABLESPOON MEDIUM-GRIND BLACK PEPPER
2 TEASPOONS SALT
1 BAY LEAF
¾ CUP KETCHUP

For the meat:

3 RACKS BABY BACK PORK RIBS (ABOUT 17–20 SMALL RIBS PER RACK)

Pork and Beans

2 TABLESPOONS OIL

1 POUND BONELESS PORK TENDER-
    LOIN, CUT INTO 1-INCH CUBES

1 YELLOW ONION, CUT INTO 1-INCH
    CHUNKS

3 STRIPS BACON, CUT INTO 1-INCH
    PIECES

¼ TEASPOON SALT

½ TEASPOON BLACK PEPPER

2 TABLESPOONS TOMATO PASTE

TWO 16-OUNCE CANS BOSTON BAKED
    BEANS

f you can buy slab bacon, substitute a scant four ounces, cut into ¼-inch dice, for the sliced bacon.

1. In a cast-iron skillet, heat the oil on medium-high until hot. Add the pork, onion, and bacon, and cook for 15 minutes.

2. Add the salt, pepper, tomato paste, and ½ cup of water. Cover and simmer for 40 minutes. Add the canned beans and simmer 5 minutes more.

SERVES 4

Penne with Tomato Salsa Sauce

"Salsa" means "sauce" in both Italian and Spanish. This south-of-the-border dish combines the familiar tomato and garlic of Italian pasta sauces with the spice and bite of Mexican salsa.

1. In a nonstick skillet over medium-high heat, cook the sausage, stirring frequently, until lightly browned, about 10 minutes. Add the garlic and cook for 1 minute.

2. In a food processor, process the tomatoes until smooth. Add the tomatoes and salsa to the sausage and cook over low heat, stirring occasionally, until reduced and slightly thickened, about 20 minutes.

3. Bring a large pot of salted water to a boil over high heat. Add the penne and quickly bring the water back to a boil. Stir the pasta a few times so it does not stick or clump together. Boil according to the manufacturer's directions but begin tasting the pasta several minutes before the suggested cooking time has elapsed. It should be tender but offer just a little resistance to your teeth.

4. When the pasta is done, drain immediately in a colander.

5. In a large bowl, toss the penne with the sauce, mozzarella cheese, and basil. Spoon into serving bowls and sprinkle with the Parmesan cheese.

SERVES 4–6

1 POUND SWEET ITALIAN SAUSAGE, CASINGS REMOVED AND CRUMBLED

1 CLOVE GARLIC, PEELED AND CRUSHED IN A GARLIC PRESS

ONE 16-OUNCE CAN PEELED TOMATOES

2 CUPS NEWMAN'S OWN SALSA OR YOUR FAVORITE

1 POUND PENNE, ROTELLE, OR ANY PASTA WITH A SHORT, STUBBY SHAPE

6 OUNCES MOZZARELLA CHEESE, SHREDDED (ABOUT 1½ CUPS), OR A COMBINATION OF MOZZARELLA AND CHEDDAR CHEESE

½ CUP CHOPPED FRESH BASIL (OPTIONAL)

GRATED PARMESAN CHEESE (OPTIONAL)

Entrance to the camp

Charlotte's Hole in the Wall Gang Camp Stuffed Shells

ONE 12-OUNCE BOX JUMBO SHELLS

ONE 10-OUNCE PACKAGE FROZEN
CHOPPED SPINACH, THAWED

1 TABLESPOON COOKING OIL

1 LARGE ONION, CHOPPED

SALT AND PEPPER TO TASTE

1 CLOVE GARLIC, MINCED

3 POUNDS RICOTTA CHEESE

ONE 26-OUNCE JAR NEWMAN'S OWN
MARINARA STYLE VENETIAN
SPAGHETTI SAUCE OR YOUR
FAVORITE (1 CUP FOR THE BAKING
DISH, THE REST FOR THE PASTA)

2 CUPS SHREDDED MOZZARELLA
CHEESE

For an adult version of these stuffed shells, add a small can of sliced mushrooms. If any of the shells break during cooking, you can serve them, unstuffed, with a little of the marinara sauce. Charlotte Werner, who cooks at the camp, serves this with garlic bread and a salad.

1. Bring a large pot of salted water to a boil over high heat. Add the pasta and quickly bring the water back to a boil. Stir the pasta a few times so it does not stick or clump together. Boil according to the manufacturer's directions, but begin tasting the pasta several minutes before the suggested cooking time has elapsed. It should be tender but offer just a little resistance to your teeth.

2. When the pasta is done, drain it in a colander and run cold water over it to stop the cooking.

3. Squeeze out the excess water from the spinach with your hands or press in a sieve with a spoon.

4. Heat the oil in a large skillet over medium-high heat. Add the onion and cook until soft. Add the spinach, salt, pepper, and garlic. Stir until mixed.

5. Place the onion mixture in a large bowl. When it is cool, add the ricotta cheese and mix well.

6. Pour 1 cup of the marinara sauce into a 13 × 9-inch glass baking pan and spread with a spoon to cover the bottom of the pan.

7. Preheat the oven to 350°F.

8. With a teaspoon, generously stuff the cheese mixture into the pasta shells. Place them in rows on top of the sauce.

9. Pour the remaining sauce over the stuffed shells. Sprinkle the mozzarella cheese on top.

10. Bake until the cheese is melted and the sauce is bubbling, about 20–30 minutes.

SERVES 8

Tim Robbins's Crunchy Oven-Fried Snapper Fillets

Crushed cornflakes give these fillets a coarse, crunchy texture; for a softer coating, omit the cornflakes and increase the quantity of bread crumbs. Cook fish about ten minutes per inch of thickness, but check at eight or nine minutes by poking a thin-bladed knife into the thickest part. If the interior is opaque and white, and the flesh has begun to flake, the fish is done. An instant-read thermometer should register 137°F.

Make fish-and-chips without all the fuss and muss of frying by pairing these fillets with "Oven-Fried" Potatoes (page 78). You can use any firm, white fish, such as orange roughy, dogfish, or halibut. Even softer fish like cod, haddock, and scrod will perform well since you don't have to turn them, flip them, or move them around much.

1. Preheat the oven to 450°F. Lightly coat a baking sheet with nonstick spray or mild-tasting vegetable oil.

2. Rinse the fillets under running water and carefully pat dry with paper towels. Cut into serving-size pieces.

3. Whir the cornflakes in a blender or food processor to make into crumbs or place in a sturdy plastic bag and crush with a rolling pin. You should have about 1 cup of cornflake crumbs.

4. Mix the cornflake crumbs, bread crumbs, salt, and pepper together, and spread in a pie plate or shallow bowl.

5. Break the eggs into another shallow bowl and beat well.

6. Dip each fillet first into the egg and then into the crumbs. Pat gently to help make the crumbs stick.

7. Roast the fillets 8–12 minutes, depending on thickness.

SERVES 4

1½–2 POUNDS RED SNAPPER FILLETS OR ANY FIRM, WHITE-FLESHED FISH THAT CAN BE CUT INTO THICK FILLETS OR STEAKS, SKIN REMOVED IF POSSIBLE
2 CUPS CORNFLAKES
1 CUP FINE DRY BREAD CRUMBS
½ TEASPOON SALT
½ TEASPOON BLACK PEPPER
3 EGGS

Southern-Style Orange Roughy Fillets

1½–2 POUNDS ORANGE ROUGHY
  FILLETS, CUT IN SERVING-SIZE
  PIECES
2 CUPS CORNMEAL
1 CUP FLOUR
½ TEASPOON SALT
1 TEASPOON BLACK PEPPER
2 TABLESPOONS FINELY CHOPPED
  PARSLEY, OR 1 TABLESPOON DRIED
  PARSLEY
3 EGGS, WELL BEATEN
2 TABLESPOONS BUTTER
2 TABLESPOONS VEGETABLE OIL

These fillets have a cornmeal coating and are lightly panfried and then baked. Refrigerating the fish fillets after they have been rolled in the cornmeal mixture helps the coating stick during the frying process. You can substitute any firm, white-fleshed fish such as dogfish, blackfish, grouper, halibut, or snapper.

For a southern-style meal, serve these fillets with Garlic Green Beans (page 81) and warm Drop Biscuits (page 42).

1. Rinse the fillets in cold water and pat dry.

2. In a flat dish or pie plate, mix together the cornmeal, flour, salt, pepper, and parsley.

3. Beat the eggs and put them in another flat dish.

4. Dip each fillet in the egg and then dredge in the cornmeal mixture. Put the breaded fillets on a cookie sheet, cover with waxed paper, and refrigerate for 30 minutes.

5. While the fillets are chilling, preheat the oven to 375°F.

6. Heat a cast-iron or other heavy nonstick skillet over medium-high heat for 3 minutes. When the skillet is hot, add the butter and oil, and heat until the butter turns golden.

7. Brown the fillets, 2 at a time, about 2–3 minutes per side, depending on their thickness. They should just begin to be flaky.

8. Remove the fillets from the skillet and pat with paper towels to remove any extra grease. Place on an ovenproof platter and bake for 5 minutes.

SERVES 4

Candice Bergen's Baked Halibut Fillets with Lemon, Peanuts, and Honey Mustard

ny firm, white-fleshed fish will be excellent in this recipe; substitute haddock, pollock, red snapper, rockfish, or scrod if you wish. Serve this flavorful dish with plain rice and plain crisp-cooked green beans.

1. Preheat the oven to 350°F. Butter a baking dish large enough to hold the halibut in 1 layer.

2. Season the halibut with salt and pepper, and rub it with the oil. Cover and refrigerate while you prepare the sauce.

3. Toast the peanuts in the oven on an ungreased pie plate about 4–5 minutes, or until golden brown and crisp. Stir them around every minute or so because they burn easily. Remove from the oven and cool. Chop them finely.

4. Mix the lemon juice, honey mustard, orange juice, salt, pepper, and oil. Stir in the peanuts.

5. Put the halibut in a buttered baking dish and bake for 15 minutes, or until the fish is white and opaque throughout and begins to flake. An instant-read thermometer inserted in the thickest part of the fish should read 137°F.

6. When the fish is done, pour the sauce over the fillets.

SERVES 4

For the fish:
1½–2 POUNDS HALIBUT FILLETS
SALT AND PEPPER TO TASTE
2 TABLESPOONS OIL

For the sauce:
½ CUP SALTED PEANUTS
¼ CUP LEMON JUICE
¼ CUP HONEY MUSTARD
½ CUP ORANGE JUICE
½ TEASPOON SALT
½ TEASPOON BLACK PEPPER
1 TABLESPOON OIL

Sarah Jessica Parker's Deviled Shrimp Salad

1 POUND SHRIMP, PRECOOKED OR RAW,
DEFROSTED (IF NECESSARY) AND
PATTED DRY WITH PAPER TOWELS
1 BAY LEAF (OPTIONAL)
5 EGGS
4 TEASPOONS PAPRIKA
½ TEASPOON SALT
½ TEASPOON BLACK PEPPER
1 TEASPOON SPIKE SEASONING
½ CUP SWEET PICKLE RELISH
4 TABLESPOONS MAYONNAISE
½ CUP DIJON MUSTARD

This elegant salad is nice for a special occasion. Although you can buy frozen precooked, peeled shrimp, you can cook and peel a pound of shrimp in not too much time. Larger shrimp are more expensive but easier to peel; smaller shrimp cost less but call for more work.

Spike seasoning is available in health food stores and some supermarkets. If you can't find it, substitute Old Bay Seafood Seasoning.

1. To cook the shrimp, bring 4 quarts of salted water to a boil. Add a bay leaf for extra flavoring. Drop the shrimp, shells and all, into the water and quickly bring back to a boil. Immediately lower to a simmer and cook the shrimp, uncovered, for 2–4 minutes, or until bright pink. They should be opaque throughout. Drain, peel off the shells, and remove the black vein with a knife. To prepare precooked frozen shrimp, simply defrost and pat dry with paper towels. Chop the shrimp finely.

2. In a saucepan, bring enough water to a boil to cover the eggs by 1 inch. Carefully lower the eggs into the water, turn down the heat, and gently boil for 14 minutes. Don't let the water boil so hard that the eggs bump together and crack.

3. As soon as the eggs are cooked, remove from the heat and plunge into a large bowl of cold water. This helps prevent a gray ring from forming around the yolk. Cool the eggs, peel them, and chop finely.

4. Mix together the shrimp, eggs, and all the other ingredients. Adjust the seasoning. Place the salad in a covered container and refrigerate.

SERVES 6

James Naughton's Creamy Baked Pasta

This easy recipe can be made entirely ahead of time. You can add more chopped tomatoes if you like. Or, for an adult version, substitute ½ cup crumbled goat cheese for the ricotta and garnish with 1 cup of shredded fresh basil leaves instead of the parsley. However you make it, this is a definite crowd pleaser.

1. Preheat the oven to 450°F. Lightly oil a 13 × 9-inch baking dish.

2. Bring a large pot of salted water to a boil over high heat. Add the pasta and quickly bring the water back to a boil. Stir the pasta a few times so it does not stick or clump together. Boil according to the manufacturer's directions but begin tasting the pasta several minutes before the suggested cooking time has elapsed. It should be tender but offer just a little resistance to your teeth.

3. When the pasta is done, drain immediately in a colander and run cold water over it to stop the cooking.

4. In a large bowl, toss the pasta with the sauce, 1 cup of the mozzarella cheese, the other cheeses, tomatoes, salt, and pepper.

5. Pour the pasta mixture into the prepared baking dish. Press the pasta down gently with a large spoon and sprinkle with the remaining 1 cup of mozzarella cheese.

6. Cover with foil and bake for 30 minutes. Remove the foil and bake 5 minutes more. Remove from the oven and cool for 10 minutes before serving. Garnish with the parsley.

SERVES 6

James Naughton and campers do an Elvis number at the Hole in the Wall Gang Camp gala

1 POUND OF YOUR FAVORITE PASTA
2 CUPS NEWMAN'S OWN "SAY CHEESE"
   PASTA SAUCE OR YOUR FAVORITE
   TOMATO-AND-CHEESE PASTA SAUCE
2 CUPS GRATED MOZZARELLA CHEESE
   (1 CUP FOR THE SAUCE, 1 CUP FOR
   THE TOPPING)
½ CUP GRATED PARMESAN CHEESE
1 CUP GRATED ASIAGO CHEESE
½ CUP GRATED ROMANO CHEESE
½ CUP RICOTTA CHEESE
½ CUP CHOPPED TOMATOES
¼ TEASPOON SALT
½ TEASPOON BLACK PEPPER
½ CUP COARSELY CHOPPED PARSLEY
   FOR GARNISH

6 EGGS
½ TEASPOON DRY MUSTARD
½ TEASPOON SALT
DASH OF PEPPER
DASH OF TABASCO SAUCE
2 CUPS MILK
6 SLICES BUTTERED BREAD
10 OUNCES SHARP CHEDDAR CHEESE,
     GRATED (ABOUT 4½ CUPS)

his is much easier than a true soufflé because all the ingredients are just layered in a pan, covered with beaten, spiced-up eggs, and baked. Start it the day before you plan to eat it because the bread and cheese have to soak in the egg mixture overnight. It makes a great brunch dish.

1. The day before: Butter a 10 × 13-inch baking dish that can go from refrigerator to oven.

2. Beat the eggs until frothy. Add the mustard, salt, pepper, Tabasco sauce, and milk.

3. Remove the crusts from the buttered bread and cut the slices into cubes.

4. Make alternate layers of bread and cheese in the baking dish. Pour the egg mixture on top. Cover and refrigerate overnight.

5. Preheat the oven to 350°F. Bake for 1 hour, or until the top is browned and the mixture is bubbling.

SERVES 6

CHAPTER 4 — Vegetables and Sides

If Your Kids Won't Eat Their Vegetables, Try . . .

Judy Collins's Brown Sugar Carrot Coins

Glenn Close's Georgia-Style "Creamed" Corn

Mashed Potatoes

Twice-Baked Potatoes

Bill Irwin's Three-Cheese Potato Gratin

"Oven-Fried" Potatoes

Cheddar Cheese Spinach

Anjelica Huston's Bandito Broccoli

Garlic Green Beans

Carole King's Green Beans with Honey Mustard and Almonds

Coleslaw

Zucchini with Mozzarella and Pretzel Crumbles

Pickled Cucumbers

Ants on a Tree (Celery and Cucumber Stuffed with Peanut Butter and Raisins)

Sweet Corn Bread

Conquering your fears is a big part of being able to do whatever you want to do. The first step is to understand exactly why the fear is there. The next step is to understand that maybe you have to have part of the fear, but maybe you can get rid of some of it. The next step is to try to destroy the root of it.

Like the first time I stood up on my prosthetics. I was scared that I was gonna fall, but then I calmed down. I realized that if I fall, big deal, I fall. My motivation was high because I knew what it was like, and I wanted to do it again. Before, I was taking advantage of being able to walk, and when I lost it, I was so sad. But when I finally stood up and walked, it was so exciting. It was like I was doing it for the very first time. I wrote a poem about it:

> **When the Tree Stands Up**
>
> When the tree stands up
> And its heart feels good
> The other trees ask, "Why are you happy?
> We're just wood."
> Before I was on the ground.
> I grabbed on to a rope of clouds
> And was pulled up.
> A vine bandaged up my roots,
> The sun sprinkled me with pines that are green all
>   year round.
> I felt like being born—
> Like being there again for the first time.

* * *

Before I saw only my bed of darkness,
Now I have owl's eyes.
Before I smelled sushi-smelling worms,
Now I smell fresh air like the sticky stuff inside of
  pine cones.
Before I heard seeds closing up, like squirrels hitting
  leaves.
Now I hear budding chirps.
Before I had cold cups of memories,
Now I have holidays of green.

I am an arm of nature.
My branches are the fingers of the forest
Stroking memories of the very first spring

Adam,
ex-camper

If Your Kids Won't Eat
Their Vegetables, Try . . .

Spices
Cinnamon
Spike seasoning
Lawry's Seasoning Salt
Salt
Chili powder
Lemon pepper

Liquid Condiments
Worcestershire sauce
Low-sodium soy sauce
Honey
Dijon mustard
Seasoned rice wine vinegar
Balsamic vinegar
Sugar (occasionally)
Newman's Own Old Fashioned Roadside
    Virgin Lemonade
Frozen limeade
Newman's Own spaghetti and pasta sauces
Newman's Own salad dressings
Butch Barbecue Sauce (see page 57)
Newman's Own salsas
Newman's Own Organic Bavarian Style
    Pretzels, crumbled

Nuts
Toffee peanuts, salted peanuts
Almonds
Macadamias
Pecans
Walnuts
Soy nuts

Cheeses
Mozzarella
Cheddar—the real thing, not processed or
    packaged as "singles"
Swiss
Parmesan
Monterey Jack
Goat

If all else fails, pour ketchup, that old favorite,
liberally over everything.

Judy Collins's Brown Sugar Carrot Coins

These caramelized sweet-and-sour carrot coins can be served warm or at room temperature. You can make them the day before and marinate them overnight to intensify the flavors.

1. Peel the carrots and cut into coins. Cook in boiling salted water until tender but still slightly crisp, about 4 minutes. Drain and pat dry with paper towels.

2. Melt the butter in a skillet over medium-high heat. Cook the carrots in the butter for about 3 minutes. Add the lemon juice, brown sugar, salt, and pepper, and stir for 1 minute or so to coat the carrots evenly.

3. Serve warm, at room temperature, or refrigerate overnight and serve cold.

SERVES 4

8 MEDIUM CARROTS
4 TABLESPOONS BUTTER
JUICE OF 2 LEMONS
2 TABLESPOONS BROWN SUGAR
SALT AND PEPPER TO TASTE

THE CHALLENGE

Keep it going
Don't stop
Keep in mind you're going to get cured
Keep on trying and don't give up
Trust your doctors and nurses and
God's help, friends, and family
As they make you laugh and
Bring cards, flowers, balloons, and candy
<u>HOPE</u> that you can make it.

Happy, glad, wonderful
Feel better than ever
No more medicine, blood transfusions
No going to the hospital for days and nights
Not throwing up
Being cured
Living your life free
Leaving it behind and starting again
<u>HOPE</u> that you're on your way!

Jovannie,
camper

Glenn Close's Georgia-Style "Creamed" Corn

This recipe contains no cream, but the long cooking time reduces the corn to a creamy texture. Use white corn if it is available, but yellow corn is fine also. Children love this southern-style dish, which goes well with pork or fried chicken.

8 EARS CORN
2 STRIPS BACON, CUT INTO ¼-INCH
    PIECES
ONE 14-OUNCE CAN CHICKEN STOCK
4 TABLESPOONS UNSALTED BUTTER
SALT AND PEPPER TO TASTE

1. Husk the corn. With the stem end of the cob resting in a large bowl, cut the raw kernels off the cobs, working from the tip down to the stem. After you have cut off the kernels, squeeze each cob hard to "milk" its juices into the bowl with the corn.

2. In a heavy 2-quart saucepan over high heat, cook the bacon for 2 minutes, stirring the pieces so they don't stick.

3. Add the corn kernels, scraping the bowl with a rubber scraper to get all the "milk" into the pan. Add the chicken stock and enough water to cover the corn by 1 inch. Cook rapidly for 15 minutes. Turn the heat to medium, add the butter, partially cover the pan, and cook 30 minutes more, stirring occasionally.

4. Season with salt and pepper. Since the bacon can be very salty, you may not have to add much salt.

SERVES 4

5 LARGE BAKING POTATOES (IDAHO OR
RUSSET), WASHED, PEELED, AND
CUT INTO 5–6 CHUNKS APIECE
4 TABLESPOONS BUTTER, SOFTENED
1½ CUPS CREAM OR MILK
SALT AND PEPPER TO TASTE

If you want to put your children's energy to good use, let them mash potatoes. This recipe calls for one of the simplest of all kitchen tools, the old-fashioned, one-piece potato masher, which yields perfect results if wielded with plenty of "elbow grease." The high starch content of baking potatoes produces the lightest, fluffiest result. Cream is delicious in mashed potatoes, but you can substitute milk to lower the fat content.

1. Put the potatoes in a large saucepan and add enough cold water to cover by 1 inch. Boil until fork-tender, about 15–20 minutes.

2. Drain the potatoes and add the butter and half of the cream, a little at a time. Mash with a hand masher. Gradually add the rest of the cream, until the potatoes have a smooth, fluffy consistency. You may need extra cream since some potatoes are starchier than others and require more liquid.

3. Season with salt and pepper. Serve immediately.

SERVES 6

Twice-Baked Potatoes

hese rich, filling potatoes will remind your children of the comforts of home long after they have grown up and gone out into the world. You can pair them with soup and salad or vegetable chili as the centerpiece of a vegetarian meal, or with roast chicken or beef for an old-fashioned meat-and-potatoes feast.

6 BAKING POTATOES (IDAHO OR RUSSET)
½ CUP GRATED CHEDDAR OR MONTEREY JACK CHEESE, SHREDDED MOZZARELLA, OR CRUMBLED GOAT CHEESE
SALT AND PEPPER TO TASTE
1 CUP MILK
¾ CUP GRATED PARMESAN CHEESE

1. Preheat the oven to 400°F.

2. With a soft vegetable brush, scrub the potatoes well under running water. Pierce in several places with a fork so they don't explode in the oven.

3. Bake until soft, 45–60 minutes, depending on the size of the potatoes. Remove from the oven.

4. When the potatoes are cool enough to handle, slice an oval flap off the top of each one. With a spoon, scoop the insides of the potato into a large bowl, leaving a shell about ½ inch thick.

5. Add the cheddar cheese, salt, and pepper to the cooked potato. Slowly add the milk, whipping the mixture with a fork until it has a firm, creamy consistency. Season with additional salt and pepper if desired.

6. Stuff the potatoes with the mixture. Sprinkle the Parmesan cheese on top.

7. Arrange the potatoes in an ovenproof dish and cover with foil. Return the dish to the oven and bake for 15 minutes, until the cheese is melted.

SERVES 6

NEVER, EVER GIVE UP!

When you feel lost,
When you feel pain,
When you feel as if you're going insane,
When you want to cry, go to sleep and close your eyes.
But you can't run away from your tears,
Wake up and face your fears.
Because when you do, and they are still there,
And it feels as if nobody cares,
And you feel so alone, as if everyone is throwing stones.
If you turn around and fight,
You will see a shining light.
When you feel upset, depressed, down on your knees,
Get up, be positive, and fight your disease.

Cathryn,
camper

Bill Irwin's Three-Cheese Potato Gratin

Bill Irwin at the 1996 camp gala

The small amount of goat cheese accents the flavors of this creamy potato gratin, but if you (or your children) don't like it, you can substitute grated cheddar.

1. Preheat the oven to 375°F. Butter an 11 × 7-inch baking dish with 1 tablespoon of the butter.

2. Peel the potatoes and cut into thin slices. Drop the slices into a bowl of cold water as you work so they will not discolor. When you have peeled all the potatoes, drain and pat dry with paper towels.

3. Make a layer of potatoes in the baking dish, using about half of the slices. Cover with half of the Parmesan cheese, half of the mozzarella, and half of the goat cheese. Dot with 1 tablespoon of butter. Season lightly with salt and pepper, and pour half of the cream evenly over the top.

4. Repeat with the remaining potatoes and cheeses. Dot with the remaining butter. Pour on the rest of the cream. Cover with foil and bake for 45 minutes. Remove the foil and bake 5 minutes more to brown the top. Remove from the oven and cool for 5 minutes before serving.

SERVES 4

3 TABLESPOONS BUTTER (1 TABLE-
    SPOON FOR GREASING THE BAKING
    DISH, THE REST FOR THE GRATIN)
4 LARGE BOILING POTATOES
1 CUP GRATED PARMESAN CHEESE
1 CUP SHREDDED MOZZARELLA
    CHEESE
¼ CUP CRUMBLED GOAT CHEESE
SALT AND PEPPER TO TASTE
½ CUP CREAM

"Oven-Fried" Potatoes

4 MEDIUM BAKING POTATOES (IDAHO
 OR RUSSET)
2 TABLESPOONS MILD-FLAVORED
 VEGETABLE OIL
SALT AND PEPPER TO TASTE
1 TEASPOON PAPRIKA

These user-friendly "unfried" French fries are easier to prepare than the usual deep-fried kind and require much less oil. You can peel the potatoes or leave the skins on. You can cut them thick or thin—into "steak fries" or traditional French fries. You can prepare them ahead and bake them later. You can reheat them even later in a toaster oven and eat them as a snack. You can even adjust the baking temperature upward if you are oven-frying fish fillets at the same time; just reduce the cooking time and keep checking the potatoes to make sure they don't burn or dry up.

1. Preheat the oven to 350°F. Lightly coat a jelly-roll pan or a shallow roasting pan with nonstick vegetable spray or a mild-tasting vegetable oil.

2. Scrub the potatoes. Peel them or not. Cut thick or thin. For steak fries, cut lengthwise into thick slices, then cut each slice lengthwise into thirds. For regular fries, cut the slices thinner and then cut each slice into fourths.

3. If you are not going to bake the potatoes immediately, drop them into a bowl of cold water so they won't discolor. When you are ready to proceed, drain and pat dry with paper towels.

4. In a medium bowl, toss the potatoes with the oil, salt, pepper, and paprika. Turn over several times with a rubber scraper until evenly coated.

5. Arrange the potatoes in a single layer on the pan. Bake until soft inside and crisp and golden brown outside, stirring and flipping them over to be sure they don't stick. Thin French fries will take about 20 minutes; steak fries will take about 40 minutes.

6. Drain on paper towels.

SERVES 4

Cheddar Cheese Spinach

This rich, seasoned spinach goes nicely with Tim Robbins's Crunchy Oven-Fried Snapper Fillets (page 61) or a simple dish of buttered pasta. Spike seasoning is available in health food stores.

1. Let the frozen spinach thaw completely, then squeeze out the excess water with a clean dishtowel, cheesecloth, or your bare hands. You want it to be very dry.
2. In a large sauté pan, heat the oil on high and sauté the garlic for 30 seconds. Add the spinach and cook for 3 minutes.
3. Add the milk and Spike seasoning. Cook, stirring frequently, until the milk is almost completely absorbed.
4. Add the butter and melt for 1 minute. Add 1 cup of the cheese. Turn off the heat as soon as you have added the cheese. Cover the pan and let the cheese melt for 1 minute.
5. Sprinkle with black pepper.
6. Serve the extra ½ cup of cheese on the side.

NOTE: This dish is easier to make with frozen spinach, but tastier with fresh. If you choose fresh spinach, you should wash it—even the "precleaned" kind—in several changes of water to get off any grit that may still cling to the leaves. Then boil it in a large pot of salted water for 2 minutes. Drain immediately in a colander, cool with cold water, and proceed as with frozen spinach.

SERVES 4

TWO 10-OUNCE PACKAGES FROZEN CHOPPED SPINACH, THAWED, OR TWO 10-OUNCE BAGS CLEANED SPINACH (SEE NOTE)
2 TABLESPOONS OLIVE OIL
½ TEASPOON CHOPPED FRESH GARLIC
1 CUP MILK
1 TEASPOON SPIKE SEASONING
2 TABLESPOONS SWEET BUTTER
1½ CUPS GRATED CHEDDAR CHEESE (1 CUP FOR THE SPINACH, ½ CUP TO SERVE ON THE SIDE)
¼ TEASPOON BLACK PEPPER

2 POUNDS BROCCOLI
½ TEASPOON SALT
1 TEASPOON LEMON PEPPER
ONE 11-OUNCE JAR NEWMAN'S OWN
   SALSA, MILD, MEDIUM, OR HOT, OR
   YOUR FAVORITE
¾ CUP SOUR CREAM
1½ CUPS GRATED CHEDDAR OR
   MONTEREY JACK CHEESE

If you don't have a store-bought steamer, you can improvise one by placing a colander in a large lidded pot. Put about an inch of water in the bottom of the pot, making sure the water does not touch the bottom of the colander. This broccoli is great with chicken, pork, beef, shrimp, salmon, or other flavorful fish.

1. Preheat the oven to 400°F.
2. Cut off and discard the tough lower ends of the broccoli stalks. Trim the individual florets into bite-sized pieces. Peel off the tough skin covering the main stalks and slice the stalks into bite-sized pieces.
3. Steam the broccoli until just soft, 3–5 minutes. Drain and place immediately in a 9 × 9-inch baking dish. Sprinkle with salt and lemon pepper.
4. Pour the salsa over the broccoli, dot with the sour cream, and cover with the cheese.
5. Bake for 8 minutes, or until the cheese is melted and bubbling.

SERVES 4

Garlic Green Beans

These southern-style beans, cooked until soft, are a great accompaniment to David Letterman's Baked Chicken in A+ Sauce (page 41). Garlic lovers can comfortably double the number of garlic cloves.

1. Wash the beans and snap off both ends. Bring a large pot of salted water to a boil. Boil the beans for 5 minutes, or until slightly crisp and still bright green. Drain in a colander and run cold water over the beans to stop the cooking.

2. Melt half of the butter in a large skillet over medium heat. Put the garlic in the skillet and cook for 3 minutes, or until just golden. Do not let the garlic brown, or it will taste bitter. (If the garlic starts to brown, remove it from the heat and set aside. Sprinkle over the top of the finished beans.)

3. Add the green beans and cook 7 minutes more. Add the water and the other half of the butter. Season with salt and pepper to taste. Cover and simmer for 10 minutes.

SERVES 6

1½ POUNDS GREEN BEANS
3 TABLESPOONS UNSALTED BUTTER
    (HALF FOR SAUTÉING THE GARLIC,
    HALF FOR COOKING THE BEANS)
3 CLOVES GARLIC, SLIVERED
¼ CUP WATER OR CHICKEN BROTH
SALT AND PEPPER TO TASTE

Carole King's Green Beans with Honey Mustard and Almonds

Carole King on the Hole in the Wall stage

1 POUND FRESH GREEN BEANS
¼ CUP HONEY MUSTARD
¼ CUP LEMON JUICE
¼ CUP WATER
½ TEASPOON SALT
½ TEASPOON BLACK PEPPER
2 TABLESPOONS BUTTER
½ CUP SLIVERED ALMONDS

These beans have lots of flavor and a crunchy texture. Serve them with something simple like Jerry Stiller's Roasted Turkey Breast (page 50) and plain rice.

1. Snap both ends off the beans. Drop them into a 5-quart saucepan of boiling salted water and cook for about 6–8 minutes, until tender but still a little crisp. Drain in a colander and immediately rinse with cold water to stop the cooking.

2. While the beans are cooking, mix the honey mustard, lemon juice, water, salt, and pepper.

3. Melt the butter in a large sauté pan over medium-high heat. Add the beans and cook for 5 minutes, stirring occasionally. Pour on the honey mustard mixture and stir again to coat the beans evenly.

4. Add the slivered almonds and cook 1 minute more.

SERVES 4

Coleslaw

This colorful coleslaw has red and green cabbage as well as red and green onions. If you like a tangier taste, add more scallions. Make the slaw at least two hours before you plan to serve it, so the flavors can mingle and develop.

1. Place the green and red cabbage in a large bowl with the scallion and onion.

2. In a small bowl, mix the mayonnaise, mustard, and vinegar. Season with salt and pepper. Pour over the vegetables and mix well.

3. Cover and refrigerate until ready to serve.

SERVES 4

2 CUPS SHREDDED GREEN CABBAGE
1 CUP SHREDDED RED CABBAGE
¼ CUP CHOPPED SCALLION, WHITE
   AND TENDER GREEN PARTS
¼ CUP CHOPPED RED ONION
½ CUP MAYONNAISE
¼ CUP HONEY MUSTARD
1 TABLESPOON VINEGAR
SALT AND PEPPER TO TASTE

When I first came here, I was bald and sick, but vibrance and enthusiasm surrounded me with songs, cheers, and smiles. After talking to a few of the kids, it didn't take long to realize that they had been through similar experiences—losing hair, missing school, getting stuck with needles, or being in the hospital. Nowhere else have I found myself with so many inspirations: campers done with chemo, getting straight A's and with full heads of hair.

Although we come from different backgrounds, families, environments, and memories, we share one common bond—hope.

Andrea,
camper

Zucchini with Mozzarella and Pretzel Crumbles

Steaming is a great way to cook vegetables because it preserves the nutrients and is easy to do. Use a purchased steamer basket or improvise your own with a colander (see page 80).

The crisp pretzel topping contrasts with the melted mozzarella cheese. You can break up the pretzels by hand or put them in a sturdy zippered plastic bag and roll a glass jar or rolling pin back and forth over them.

1. Preheat the oven to 400°F. Lightly butter a 9 × 13-inch baking dish or ovenproof casserole.

2. Scrub the zucchini and summer squash carefully under running water until no dirt remains on the skin. Cut the squashes crosswise into ½-inch slices.

3. Put ¾ inch of water in a large pot. Steam the zucchini and summer squash until just soft, about 6 minutes. Remove to the baking dish and sprinkle with the salt, lemon pepper, and cumin.

4. Sprinkle the pretzel crumbles over the vegetables. Drizzle the oil over the top. Sprinkle the cheese on top of everything.

5. Bake for 8–10 minutes, or until the cheese is bubbling.

SERVES 4

2 MEDIUM GREEN ZUCCHINI
2 MEDIUM YELLOW SUMMER SQUASH
½ TEASPOON SALT
1 TEASPOON LEMON PEPPER
¼ TEASPOON CUMIN
1 CUP CRUMBLED NEWMAN'S OWN ORGANIC BAVARIAN STYLE PRETZELS OR YOUR FAVORITE
2 TABLESPOONS EXTRA-VIRGIN OLIVE OIL
1 CUP SHREDDED SMOKED MOZZARELLA CHEESE

Pickled Cucumbers

1 HOTHOUSE CUCUMBER

¼ CUP VERY THINLY SLICED YELLOW
   ONION

¼ CUP TOASTED SESAME SEEDS (SEE
   NOTE)

½–¾ CUP SEASONED RICE WINE
   VINEGAR

For this recipe use a hothouse (also known as "burpless" or European) cucumber. These cucumbers are long and skinny and have very small seeds and bumpy skin; they are often packaged in plastic wrap.

1. Scrub the cucumber under running water and slice it very thinly.

2. Combine the cucumber, onion, and sesame seeds in a medium bowl. Pour on ½ cup of seasoned rice wine vinegar. Add more if necessary, until the cucumber slices are almost covered; they should not be entirely immersed in the vinegar. Marinate at least 2 hours before serving.

NOTE: If you can find Japanese toasted sesame seeds in your supermarket, by all means use them. Otherwise use regular sesame seeds and toast them at 350°F in your oven or toaster oven for about 5–6 minutes, until golden brown. Watch them carefully and stir them occasionally so they don't burn.

SERVES 6

Ants on a Tree

(Celery and Cucumber Stuffed with Peanut Butter
and Raisins)

Adults might prefer goat cheese or a mixture of cream cheese and blue cheese as a stuffing for celery or cucumber sticks, but children are bound to go for this peanut butter filling stuck with raisins.

1. Peel the cucumbers, slice them in half lengthwise, and scrape out the seeds with a sharp spoon. If they are large, cut into bite-sized pieces. Or trim the ends of the celery stalks, cut in half crosswise, and pull off any tough strings.

2. Spread 1 tablespoon of peanut butter in each cucumber or celery piece. Stick raisins into the peanut butter to make the "ants."

SERVES 6

3 SMALL CUCUMBERS, OR 6 STALKS
   CELERY
¾ CUP (12 TABLESPOONS) PEANUT
   BUTTER
¼ CUP RAISINS

Sweet Corn Bread

1 TABLESPOON VEGETABLE OIL

1 TABLESPOON UNSALTED BUTTER

1 CUP FRESH OR FROZEN CORN,
   THAWED

1½ CUPS YELLOW CORNMEAL

½ CUP FLOUR

1 TEASPOON BAKING POWDER

½ TEASPOON BAKING SODA

1 TABLESPOON SUGAR

¼ TEASPOON ONION POWDER
   (OPTIONAL)

2 EGGS, BEATEN

1 CUP BUTTERMILK

½ TEASPOON SALT

¾ TEASPOON BLACK PEPPER

This corn bread is best with fresh corn, though you can make it with frozen corn. Spoon pork and beans over it for a homey supper or bake it in muffin tins and serve as a snack. If you decide to make muffins, bake them for about twelve minutes; a toothpick inserted in the middle of a muffin should come out clean.

1. Preheat the oven to 350°F. Grease a 9 × 9-inch baking dish.

2. Heat the oil and butter in a skillet on low heat until the butter is melted. Add the corn and cook for about 5 minutes, until soft.

3. In a medium bowl, mix the cornmeal, flour, baking powder, baking soda, sugar, onion powder, eggs, buttermilk, salt, and pepper. Add the cooked corn and stir to mix.

4. Pour into the prepared baking dish and bake for 40 minutes, or until the top is lightly browned.

SERVES 4

Nachos with Guacamole, Salsa, and Monterey Jack Cheese

Cinnamon-Sugar Pizza

Sweet and Savory Cheddar Muffins

Grandma's Banana Bread

Raisin-Walnut Snack Cake

Super Second Grade Popcorn and Peanuts

Colonel Pop's Fun Friday Popcorn Pops

Newman's Own Sweet New England Popcorn

Fast Eddie's Fast-Disappearing Apricot Popcorn Balls

Nachos with Guacamole, Salsa, and Monterey Jack Cheese

For the guacamole:

3 RIPE AVOCADOS
1 TABLESPOON FINELY CHOPPED
    YELLOW ONION
1 TEASPOON SALT
1 JALAPEÑO CHILE, SEEDS AND VEINS
    REMOVED AND FINELY CHOPPED
    (OPTIONAL)

For the nachos:

ONE 14-OUNCE BAG BLUE CORN
    TORTILLA CHIPS
2 CUPS GRATED MONTEREY JACK
    CHEESE
1 CUP NEWMAN'S OWN SALSA, MILD,
    MEDIUM, OR HOT, OR YOUR
    FAVORITE
½ CUP SOUR CREAM

If you have a mortar and pestle, use them to mash the ingredients for the guacamole, working in batches. A large fork will also do the trick. Or you can mash the avocados, onion, salt, and pepper together with your (very clean) bare hands and stir in the optional chopped jalapeño with a spoon.

Be careful when you work with hot chilies. Never touch your eyes after handling them. If you have sensitive skin, wear rubber gloves. And be sure to wash your hands when you are finished.

These nachos look great mounded like a small mountain on a large, oval, ovenproof platter, but a shallow casserole is also okay. Serve them at a children's party and let the children help in the preparation. For an adult version, substitute a serrano chile for the jalapeño.

1. Preheat the oven to 400°F.

2. Mash together the avocados, onion, and salt until the guacamole has a slightly chunky consistency. Stir in the jalapeño. Cover the guacamole tightly with plastic wrap and refrigerate it unless you are going to use it immediately. It will turn brown if exposed too long to the air.

3. Place a thin layer of chips on a platter. Cover with ¾ cup of the cheese and dot with ⅓ cup or more of the guacamole. Repeat 2 more times, ending with the guacamole. Depending on the size of the avocados, you may have leftover guacamole.

4. Bake for about 5 minutes, or until the cheese is melted. Serve with the salsa and sour cream on top.

SERVES 4–6

Cinnamon-Sugar Pizza

For a real treat, serve this with hot cocoa for break-fast. Or try it as an after-school snack or a simple dessert. If you use a prebaked crust, make sure it isn't flavored with olive oil or Italian seasonings.

1. Preheat the oven to 450°F.

2. Prepare and shape the pizza dough according to the manufacturer's instructions. If you are using raw dough, partially prebake it for 3–4 minutes, or until pale brown and lightly crusted on top.

3. Mix the melted butter with the sugar and cinnamon. Brush the pizza dough generously with the mixture.

4. Bake for 6-10 minutes, until crispy. Cut into 6 pieces.

SERVES 6

1 PLAIN PIZZA CRUST, 12–13 INCHES IN
    DIAMETER (SEE THE INTRODUCTION
    TO CY COLEMAN'S BARBECUE
    CHEESEBURGER PIZZA, PAGE 36)
½ CUP MELTED UNSALTED BUTTER
¼ CUP SUGAR
¼ CUP GROUND CINNAMON

This is a place where you
Can let your mind run free
A place where all the people around
Take you in
Like one of their own
They give you love
They show you how to listen with your soul
To love with your mind
To speak with your hands
And to see with your heart

Samantha,
camper

Sweet and Savory Cheddar Muffins

Don't overbeat muffin batter, or you will end up with tough, lopsided muffins. These muffins are great as a snack or with poultry dishes.

1. Preheat the oven to 350°F. Coat a 12-cup muffin tin or two 6-cup muffin tins with butter or nonstick vegetable spray.

2. In a medium bowl, mix the flours, baking soda, baking powder, salt, and pepper together with a fork. Make sure they are evenly mixed.

3. Combine the mustard and honey in a small dish, stirring with a fork until well mixed.

4. In a large bowl, beat the egg, buttermilk, milk, and cheese. Set aside 2 tablespoons of the honey-mustard mixture for the muffin tops. Add the rest to the egg mixture and stir to combine well.

5. Add the dry ingredients to the wet ingredients, stirring or folding gently until barely mixed. The batter should be a little lumpy.

6. Spoon the batter into the muffin tins, filling them ¾ full. Bake in the center of the oven for 15–20 minutes, or until a toothpick inserted in the center comes out clean and dry.

7. Cool 5 minutes before removing from the tins, loosening with a knife if necessary. Gently brush the remaining honey-mustard mixture on the tops.

MAKES 12 MUFFINS

¾ CUP WHOLE WHEAT PASTRY FLOUR
1½ CUPS UNBLEACHED WHITE FLOUR
1 TEASPOON BAKING SODA
1 TEASPOON BAKING POWDER
½ TEASPOON SALT
½ TEASPOON PEPPER
5 TABLESPOONS GRAINY MUSTARD
¼ CUP HONEY
1 EGG
½ CUP BUTTERMILK
¾ CUP MILK
1 CUP GRATED CHEDDAR CHEESE

2 CUPS FLOUR

1 TEASPOON SALT

1 TEASPOON BAKING SODA

1 CUP SUGAR

1 STICK (8 TABLESPOONS) UNSALTED
  BUTTER, SOFTENED

2 LARGE EGGS

3 VERY RIPE SMALL BANANAS, MASHED

1 CUP COARSELY CHOPPED WALNUTS

oist and succulent, this old-fashioned bread would keep well if it weren't so good to eat.

1. Preheat the oven to 350°F. Grease and flour a 9 × 5-inch loaf pan.

2. In a medium bowl, combine the flour, salt, and baking soda. Stir until well blended.

3. In a large bowl, beat the sugar and butter on medium speed of an electric mixer or by hand until light in color and creamy in texture.

4. Gradually beat the eggs into the sugar and butter on low speed.

5. Sift the dry ingredients into the wet ingredients and, using a rubber scraper or a wooden spoon, stir until blended.

6. Gently stir or fold the mashed bananas and walnuts into the batter, mixing until just combined. Do not overmix, or the banana bread will be rubbery.

7. Bake for 45–55 minutes, or until a toothpick inserted in the center of the loaf comes out clean.

8. Remove to a rack to cool. Let the bread rest for 30 minutes before serving.

SERVES 10

Raisin-Walnut Snack Cake

ot too sweet, and rich in nuts, raisins, and apple-sauce, this old-fashioned cake makes a fine afternoon snack. Use homemade applesauce if you can and add the optional ginger for extra zing.

1. Preheat the oven to 350°F. Butter and flour a 10-inch Bundt pan or a 9 × 13-inch rectangular baking dish.

2. In a large bowl, beat together the sugar and butter on medium speed of an electric mixer until light and fluffy. Beat in the eggs until thoroughly mixed.

3. In a medium bowl, mix the flour, baking soda, cinnamon, ginger, and salt with a fork until evenly combined.

4. With a rubber spatula or a mixer on low speed, mix the dry ingredients into the wet ingredients in 3 batches, alternating with the applesauce. Scrape the sides of the bowl occasionally and mix only until the dry ingredients are incorporated. Stir in the raisins and walnuts.

5. Spoon into the prepared pan and tap the pan on the table to level the batter.

6. Bake for 45–55 minutes for the Bundt pan or 35–45 minutes for the rectangular pan, or until a toothpick inserted in the center of the cake comes out clean. Cool in the pan on a rack for 10 minutes. Remove the cake from the pan and cool completely on a rack.

SERVES 12 GENEROUSLY

1 CUP PACKED DARK BROWN SUGAR
1½ STICKS (12 TABLESPOONS) BUTTER, SOFTENED
2 LARGE EGGS
3 CUPS SIFTED FLOUR
2 TEASPOONS BAKING SODA
2 TEASPOONS GROUND CINNAMON
1 TEASPOON POWDERED GINGER (OPTIONAL)
½ TEASPOON SALT
1¾ CUPS APPLESAUCE (ONE 16-OUNCE JAR)
1 CUP RAISINS
1 CUP COARSELY CHOPPED WALNUTS

Super Second Grade Popcorn and Peanuts

THREE 3.5-OUNCE BAGS NEWMAN'S OWN OLDSTYLE PICTURE SHOW MICROWAVE POPCORN, ALL NATURAL FLAVOR, OR YOUR FAVORITE

ONE 12-OUNCE BAG ROASTED PEANUTS

1 CUP BROWN SUGAR

1 STICK (8 TABLESPOONS) BUTTER OR MARGARINE

¼ CUP LIGHT CORN SYRUP

½ TEASPOON SALT

½ TEASPOON BAKING SODA

A second grade class from Annunciation School in Havelock, North Carolina, invented this snack, which is as much fun to make as it is to eat. The children donated their winnings to their school.

1. Pop the microwave popcorn according to package instructions.

2. Shell the peanuts. Put the popcorn and peanuts into a large brown paper bag.

3. Combine the remaining ingredients in a microwave-safe bowl. Cook for 2 minutes in the microwave on high power and pour into the bag. Close the bag tightly, shake thoroughly, and then eat.

SERVES 20 CHILDREN AS A SNACK

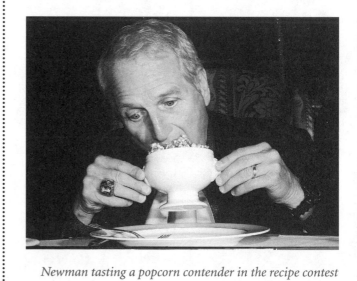

Newman tasting a popcorn contender in the recipe contest

Colonel Pop's Fun Friday Popcorn Pops

Chris Jordan, a special education teacher at Centerville Elementary School in Lilburn, Georgia, motivates her students by having "Fun Fridays," featuring games and snacks. These sweet popcorn treats, molded in cups and stuck on lollipop sticks, make any day Fun Friday. Ms. Jordan donated her charity award to the Gwinnett County Special Education Enrichment Fund.

1. Coat a large bowl with nonstick cooking spray.

2. In a 4-quart saucepan, heat the marshmallows and margarine over low heat until melted.

3. Put the popcorn in the greased bowl and pour the melted marshmallow mixture over it. Stir well to coat all the popcorn. Stir in the peanuts, Reese's Pieces, and chocolate chips.

4. Press the mixture into the cold drink cups, filling them about ¾ full. Place a wooden stick in the center of each, like a lollipop stick. Set the pops aside to cool, about 5 minutes.

5. To remove the pops, press on the bottoms of the cups.

MAKES 10 POPS

For the popcorn treats:
5½ CUPS MINIATURE MARSHMALLOWS
½ STICK (4 TABLESPOONS) MARGARINE OR BUTTER
5 CUPS POPPED NEWMAN'S OWN OLDSTYLE PICTURE SHOW POPCORN OR YOUR FAVORITE
1 CUP PEANUTS
1 CUP REESE'S PIECES
1 CUP SEMISWEET CHOCOLATE CHIPS

To form the "pops":
TEN 5-OUNCE WAX-COATED COLD DRINK CUPS
10 WOODEN ICE CREAM OR CRAFT STICKS

Newman's Own Sweet New England Popcorn

2 CUPS COARSELY CHOPPED WALNUTS
ONE 3.5-OUNCE BAG NEWMAN'S OWN
    OLDSTYLE PICTURE SHOW MICRO-
    WAVE POPCORN, ALL-NATURAL
    FLAVOR, OR YOUR FAVORITE
¾ CUP DRIED CRANBERRIES
1½ STICKS (12 TABLESPOONS) BUTTER
1½ CUPS PURE MAPLE SYRUP
½ CUP LIGHT CORN SYRUP
1 TEASPOON PUMPKIN PIE SPICE

Lori Welander, from Shelburne, Vermont, developed this sweet and savory popcorn, which contains pure maple syrup, dried cranberries, and walnuts. It is certain to evoke thoughts of autumn in New England. Ms. Welander donated her charity award to the Burlington Emergency Shelter.

Boiling sugar syrup gets very hot, so make these popcorn balls under adult supervision. If you don't have a candy thermometer for measuring the temperature of the boiling syrup, use the old-fashioned cold water test, which gives reasonably accurate results. Remove the pan from the heat during the test. Spoon out about ½ teaspoon of the syrup and drop it into a cup of cold water. Let the syrup get cold, take it out of the water with your fingers, and feel it to determine if it has reached the soft crack stage. The syrup should make hard threads that remain flexible when you take them out of the water.

1. Preheat the oven to 350°F. Spray a very large bowl with nonstick cooking spray. Grease a 15 × 10-inch roasting pan.

2. Spread the chopped walnuts in a 13 × 9-inch baking pan and toast 8–10 minutes, stirring occasionally, until lightly browned. Watch them carefully so they don't burn. Remove from the oven and set aside to cool.

3. Pop the popcorn according to package directions. Combine the popcorn, toasted walnuts, and dried cranberries in the prepared bowl and set aside.

4. In a heavy 3-quart saucepan over medium heat, melt the butter. Add the maple syrup and corn syrup and cook, stirring occasionally, until the syrup mixture registers 275°F on a candy thermometer (or reaches the soft crack stage), about 20 minutes. Remove from the heat and stir in the pumpkin pie spice.

5. Immediately pour the hot syrup over the popcorn mixture, stirring well until the popcorn is evenly coated. Pour into the prepared roasting pan and cool the pan on a wire rack. Break into pieces to serve. Store in an airtight container.

SERVES 8

Fast Eddie's Fast-Disappearing Apricot Popcorn Balls

ONE 3.5-OUNCE BAG NEWMAN'S OWN
   OLDSTYLE PICTURE SHOW MICRO-
   WAVE POPCORN, ALL NATURAL
   FLAVOR, OR YOUR FAVORITE
2 CUPS CHOPPED DRIED APRICOTS
1 CUP QUICK-COOKING (NOT INSTANT)
   OATMEAL FLAKES
1 CUP BROWN SUGAR
1 STICK (8 TABLESPOONS) UNSALTED
   BUTTER OR MARGARINE
½ CUP LIGHT CORN SYRUP

Elizabeth Cheshire of Tustin, California, who created this quick and easy recipe with her nieces and nephew, donated her charity award to the Foster Grandparent Program.

Boiling sugar syrup gets very hot, so make these popcorn balls under adult supervision. If you don't have a candy thermometer, test the temperature of the syrup using the old-fashioned cold water test, which gives fairly accurate results. Remove the pan from the heat during the test. Fill a cup with cold water. Spoon out about ½ teaspoon of the hot syrup and drop it into the water. Let the syrup get cold, remove it from the water with your fingers, and feel it. The syrup has reached the soft crack stage (270–290°F) when it makes hard threads that are still flexible. Use a fresh cup of cold water for every test.

1. Butter a large roasting pan or bowl.
2. Pop the popcorn according to the package instructions. You should have about 10 cups. Pour the popcorn into the prepared pan. Stir in the apricots and oatmeal.
3. In a 2-quart saucepan over medium heat, combine the brown sugar, butter, and corn syrup, stirring constantly. Continue cooking and stirring until the mixture reaches 290°F on a candy thermometer.
4. Pour over the popcorn mixture and stir until the popcorn is evenly coated.
5. When the mixture is cool enough to handle, form it into balls. Cool completely and store in an airtight container.

MAKES TWENTY-FOUR 3-INCH BALLS

CHAPTER 6 Desserts

Fruit Salad

Phoebe Snow's Mashed Maple Syrup Apples

Ann Reinking's Brown Sugar Rice Pudding

Chocolate Banana Bread Pudding

Rosemary Clooney's Two-Fisted Chocolate Chip Cookies

Peanut Butter Chocolate Chip Cookies

Lemon Squares

Michael Bolton's White Chocolate Brownie Hot Fudge Sundae

Newman's Very Own Lemon Blueberry Cake with Lemon Sauce

Whipped Cream–Filled Banana Cake

Whoopi Goldberg's Classic American Carrot Cake with a Twist

Dad's Favorite Chocolate-Orange Angel Food Cake

2 CUPS DICED PINEAPPLE

2 LARGE ORANGES, PEELED AND CUT
   INTO BITE-SIZED PIECES (ABOUT
   2 CUPS), JUICE RESERVED

2 CUPS RASPBERRIES

2 CUPS HALVED GRAPES

2 LARGE BANANAS, DICED
   (ABOUT 2 CUPS)

4 TABLESPOONS SWEET CLOVER OR
   OTHER MILD HONEY

JUICE OF 2 LEMONS

Buy navel oranges if you can because they are easy to peel. If you plan to serve the salad later, peel and dice the bananas at the last minute, since they will darken in the refrigerator. If you don't want to peel a fresh pineapple, you can substitute canned pineapple in juice, not syrup.

1. If using fresh pineapple, cut off the leaves. Slice off the rind at the base, so that the pineapple will stand up. Starting at the top and working down, slice off the skin in strips, cutting off as little flesh as possible. With a small knife or the pointed end of a vegetable peeler, carve out any remaining "eyes." Quarter the pineapple lengthwise and remove the core. Cut the fruit into small strips and then into cubes. Reserve the juice. If you are using canned pineapple, drain and reserve the juice. Cut into bite-sized pieces.

2. Put all the ingredients, including the reserved juice, in a bowl and mix gently so that the fruit is evenly coated with honey. Cover and chill in the refrigerator.

SERVES 6

Five summers ago I came to the Hole in the Wall for the first time. I was a short-haired twelve-year-old suffering from non-Hodgkins lymphoma and undergoing chemotherapy. It wasn't until my second year that I realized the friends I made here were unlike my friends anywhere else. I had the best summer of my life—until the next summer came, and that was the best. And the next—and that was the best. So it has been for the past five summers. But now I am well and this was my last summer and my best summer in this place that has become such a stronghold in my life. This isn't a camp <u>about</u> sick children. <u>For</u> sick children, yes. But once you drive through those gates, that's not what it's about at all. It's about life. A life that all of the campers never got to lead anywhere else, and hopefully most of the children of the world will never have to face. This camp is a nest where I hatched my personality and my life. I love this place and the people that represent it, and from this point on, no matter where I go or what I do, Hole in the Wall will be there with me.

Norah,
ex-camper

Phoebe Snow's Mashed Maple Syrup Apples

4 RED DELICIOUS APPLES
½ CUP MAPLE SYRUP
¾ CUP COARSELY CHOPPED WALNUTS
¼ CUP MELTED BUTTER
1 TEASPOON GROUND CINNAMON
1 TABLESPOON SUGAR

Serve this simple, homey dessert with vanilla frozen yogurt or ice cream, or garnish it with powdered sugar. Make sure you use Red Delicious apples, since other varieties behave differently when baked.

1. Preheat the oven to 400°F. Use a small, unbuttered baking dish for baking the apples and a 9 × 4-inch loaf pan for the mashed mixture.

2. Peel the apples and core them, using an apple corer, but leave them whole. Place them close together in the baking dish. Add ½ inch of water and bake until very soft, about 1 hour. Remove from the oven and let cool.

3. Place in a medium bowl.

4. Turn on the broiler to high.

5. While the broiler is heating, add the maple syrup, walnuts, butter, and cinnamon to the apples. Mash everything together with a large fork. Scrape the mixture into the baking dish. Sprinkle the sugar on top.

6. Broil until the top has caramelized to a rich brown, about 3 minutes.

SERVES 4

Ann Reinking's Brown Sugar Rice Pudding

The dried red cherries flecking this creamy dessert give this old favorite a new look, but you can substitute raisins if cherries are unavailable. Use sweet dried cherries, not the tart kind.

1. Preheat the oven to 325°F. Butter a 1½-quart baking dish.

2. In a saucepan, heat the water and lemon juice to boiling. Remove from the heat and drop in the dried cherries. Let them sit for 3 minutes to absorb the liquid and plump up.

3. Combine the rice, milk, sugar, and salt. Bake in the prepared baking dish for 1 hour, stirring often so the rice doesn't settle to the bottom. Stir in the lemon rind, cinnamon, and cherries.

4. Return the dish to the oven and bake 1½ hours more, or until the milk has been absorbed.

Serves 6

1¾ CUPS WATER
¼ CUP LEMON JUICE
1 CUP DRIED CHERRIES
½ CUP UNCOOKED RICE
4 CUPS MILK
⅔ CUP LIGHT BROWN SUGAR
½ TEASPOON SALT
RIND OF ½ LEMON, FINELY CHOPPED
¼ TEASPOON GROUND CINNAMON

1 LOAF HIGH-QUALITY FRENCH BREAD,
　　BAGUETTE SIZE
1 STICK (8 TABLESPOONS) CHILLED
　　BUTTER
8 EGGS
¾ CUP SUGAR
1 QUART CREAM
1 QUART MILK
1 TABLESPOON VANILLA EXTRACT
1 CUP MILK CHOCOLATE CHIPS PLUS
　　MORE FOR GARNISH
1 LARGE BANANA, SLICED LENGTHWISE
　　INTO QUARTERS AND THEN DICED
¾ CUP CHOPPED WALNUTS
2 PINTS VANILLA FROZEN YOGURT OR
　　ICE CREAM, OR 1 PINT HEAVY
　　CREAM, WHIPPED AND LIGHTLY
　　SWEETENED
POWDERED SUGAR FOR GARNISH

Serve this rich pudding in small portions topped with vanilla frozen yogurt, ice cream, or whipped cream. It reheats well in the microwave. You will need a 13 × 9-inch nonstick pan.

1. Preheat the oven to 400°F.

2. Cut the loaf of bread in half lengthwise and then cut each half lengthwise again. Cut the long pieces into 1-inch chunks.

3. Chop the butter into pieces about the size of chocolate chips.

4. In a large bowl, beat the eggs, then add the sugar, cream, butter, milk, vanilla extract, chocolate chips, banana, and walnuts. Add the bread chunks and toss well with your hands. Make sure the bread is well soaked with the liquid mixture. If it is dry, add a little more milk.

5. Place all the ingredients in the baking pan, pressing down slightly. Cover with foil and bake for 45–60 minutes. Check after 40 minutes to see whether the center of the pudding is still runny. If it is, then remove the foil and bake about 5 minutes more, until it sets. The pudding should be moist in the center because it will continue to cook after you have removed it from the oven. Cool on a rack for 15 minutes before serving.

6. While the pudding is still warm, scoop small portions onto individual plates. Spoon the frozen yogurt on top. Garnish with extra chocolate chips and sprinkle liberally with powdered sugar. Dust the plate rims with extra powdered sugar.

SERVES 8–10 GENEROUSLY

Rosemary Clooney's Two-Fisted Chocolate Chip Cookies

If you like to work with your hands, make these cookies barehanded. If you are uncomfortable about handling raw dough, use a heavy-duty mixer, but the cookies will be flatter. The three sticks of butter in the recipe will produce firm cookies; add a fourth for the traditional melt-in-your-mouth kind, but space the dough farther apart on the baking sheets.

Toast the nuts first if you decide to use them; for directions, see page 98.

1. Preheat the oven to 350°F.
2. To make the cookies by hand, put all the ingredients in a large bowl and mash together with your hands. To make the cookies with a mixer, beat the butter on medium speed until light in color and creamy. Beat in the sugars, eggs, and vanilla extract until well blended.
3. Mix together the flour, baking powder, and baking soda. On low speed gradually add the flour mixture to the butter mixture until the ingredients are just combined. By hand, stir in the milk chocolate and white chocolate chips and the nuts.
4. Drop the cookies by heaping tablespoonfuls onto ungreased cookie sheets, about 2 inches apart. For jumbo cookies, make 12 cookies per sheet.
5. Bake for 10–14 minutes, or until the cookies are golden and the edges are just browned. Remove from the oven and cool on racks. These are so good that they will disappear immediately, although you can put them out of sight and out of mind by storing them, covered, in the refrigerator.

MAKES 24 JUMBO COOKIES OR 32–48 SMALLER ONES

3 STICKS (24 TABLESPOONS) BUTTER, AT ROOM TEMPERATURE
½ CUP GRANULATED SUGAR
½ CUP BROWN SUGAR
4 EGGS, LIGHTLY BEATEN
1 TEASPOON VANILLA EXTRACT
5¼ CUPS FLOUR
1 TEASPOON BAKING POWDER
1 TEASPOON BAKING SODA
½ CUP MILK CHOCOLATE CHIPS
½ CUP WHITE CHOCOLATE CHIPS
½ CUP TOASTED AND COARSELY CHOPPED MACADAMIA NUTS, WALNUTS, OR PECANS (OPTIONAL)

Peanut Butter Chocolate Chip Cookies

1¾ CUPS SIFTED FLOUR

¼ TEASPOON SALT

¾ TEASPOON BAKING SODA

¼ TEASPOON BAKING POWDER

½ CUP CHUNKY PEANUT BUTTER

1 STICK (8 TABLESPOONS) BUTTER, SOFTENED

¼ TEASPOON VANILLA EXTRACT

½ CUP FIRMLY PACKED LIGHT BROWN SUGAR

½ CUP WHITE SUGAR

2 LARGE EGGS

1 CUP MILK CHOCOLATE CHIPS

1 CUP CHOPPED TOFFEE-COATED PEANUTS

These cookies contain two all-time favorite ingredients: peanut butter and chocolate. For extra measure they are studded with chopped toffee-coated peanuts.

1. Preheat the oven to 350°F. Line 2 cookie sheets with foil, shiny side up, or cover them with parchment paper.

2. Sift together the flour, salt, baking soda, and baking powder. Set aside.

3. In a large bowl, beat together the peanut butter, butter, and vanilla extract with a wooden spoon until soft and smooth.

4. Mix in the brown and white sugars, but don't beat. Add the eggs and mix in with the spoon. Gradually add the sifted dry ingredients, mixing in until just combined. Overworking the dough toughens it.

5. Stir in the chocolate chips and toffee peanuts.

6. Drop the dough by teaspoonfuls onto the prepared cookie sheets about 2 inches apart. With a wet spoon, gently flatten each mound of dough until it is about ½ inch thick. Bake, one pan at a time, in the middle of the oven for 7–8 minutes, until the edges are just browned.

7. Remove from the oven and cool on a rack until completely cool, about 20 minutes, before removing the cookies from the pans.

MAKES ABOUT 3 DOZEN SMALL COOKIES

Lemon Squares

These cookies have a crumbly shortbread crust covered by a tart lemon filling. They can be topped off, if you like, with a dollop of softly whipped cream. You can make an adult version of this dessert by substituting a tablespoon of Grand Marnier liqueur for the orange extract.

The shortbread has only three ingredients: flour, sugar, and butter. Start with cold butter and blend it into the flour with a pastry blender. If the mixture doesn't come together as a dough, you may have to work it with your hands until you can pat it into the baking dish.

1. Preheat the oven to 325°F.

2. To MAKE THE CRUST: In a medium bowl, stir together the flour and powdered sugar. Cut the cold butter into small pieces and blend into the dry ingredients with a pastry blender, a fork, or 2 knives. The flour and butter should blend into flakes about the size of bran flakes.

3. Pat the mixture carefully into a 9 × 13-inch baking dish. Bake for 30 minutes, until a rich golden color. Remove from the oven and cool on a rack.

4. To MAKE THE FILLING: In a medium bowl, whisk together the eggs, lemon juice, orange extract, and sugar. Stir in the flour and baking powder until well combined.

5. Pour the filling onto the crust and spread evenly. Bake for 30 minutes. Open the oven door and check the filling: It is done when the edges are set and the center is just a little bit jiggly.

6. Remove from the oven and sprinkle generously with powdered sugar. Cut into squares while still warm.

7. Whip the cream until soft peaks form. Place a dollop on each square before serving.

MAKES 24 SQUARES

For the crust:

2 CUPS FLOUR
½ CUP POWDERED SUGAR
2 STICKS (16 TABLESPOONS) COLD
    UNSALTED BUTTER

For the filling:

4 EGGS, LIGHTLY BEATEN
5 TABLESPOONS LEMON JUICE
1 TEASPOON ORANGE EXTRACT
2 CUPS SUGAR
⅓ CUP FLOUR
½ TEASPOON BAKING POWDER
POWDERED SUGAR FOR GARNISH
¾ CUP WHIPPING CREAM (OPTIONAL)

Michael Bolton's White Chocolate Brownie Hot Fudge Sundae

For the brownies:
2 OUNCES WHITE CHOCOLATE,
    COARSELY CHOPPED, OR ⅓ CUP
    WHITE CHOCOLATE CHIPS
1 STICK (8 TABLESPOONS) UNSALTED
    BUTTER
2 EGGS
1 CUP SUGAR
½ TEASPOON VANILLA EXTRACT
½ CUP FLOUR
¼ TEASPOON SALT
1 CUP CHOPPED ALMONDS (OPTIONAL)

For the sundaes:
1 CUP HOT FUDGE
4 LARGE SCOOPS VANILLA FROZEN
    YOGURT
¾ CUP CHOPPED ALMONDS
POWDERED SUGAR FOR GARNISH

This easy variation of a classic American favorite rests on a homemade white brownie and continues upward with frozen vanilla yogurt or ice cream, hot fudge, chopped almonds, and a final sprinkling of powdered sugar. You can improvise a double boiler by fitting a ceramic or stainless steel bowl into the top of a saucepan. The bottom of the bowl should be two or three inches above the bottom of the pan. The recipe makes eight brownies; wrap the extra four in foil and take them to school in your lunch box.

1. Preheat the oven to 325°F. Grease and flour an 8 × 8-inch ovenproof dish.

2. TO MAKE THE BROWNIES: In a double boiler with 1 inch of water in the bottom, melt the white chocolate with the butter, stirring constantly until the mixture is smooth. Let cool for 3 minutes. Beat in the eggs, sugar, and vanilla extract. Stir in the flour, salt, and almonds until just combined.

3. With a rubber spatula, scrape the batter into the prepared baking dish. Spread into the corners. Bake for 40 minutes, or until a toothpick inserted in the center comes out clean but a little moist. Remove from the oven to a rack and cool before cutting into bars.

4. TO ASSEMBLE THE SUNDAES: Warm the hot fudge sauce on the stove or in the microwave. If it came in a jar, set the jar (with the lid removed) in a saucepan with 1½ inches of simmering water and warm over low heat. Place a brownie in the center of each dessert plate and cover with a scoop of frozen yogurt.

5. Pour ¼ cup of hot fudge over the frozen yogurt and sprinkle with the almonds and powdered sugar.

MAKES 8 LARGE BROWNIES FOR 4 SUNDAES AND 4 EXTRA

Newman's Very Own Lemon Blueberry Cake with Lemon Sauce

Ann Marshall of Hudson, Massachusetts, submitted this recipe, which gets its lemony flavor from lemonade. She donated her charity award to the Make a Wish Foundation.

1. Preheat the oven to 350°F. Grease a 9 × 9-inch baking pan.

2. In a large bowl, beat together the shortening and sugar on medium-high speed of an electric mixer until light and fluffy. Add the eggs, one at a time, beating well after each addition. Stir in the lemon extract and lemonade.

3. In a separate bowl, stir together the flour, baking powder, and salt. Add to the shortening-egg mixture, alternating with the milk. Beat well after each addition. The batter should be smooth.

4. Sprinkle the blueberries in the bottom of the prepared baking pan. Reserve ½ cup of the cake batter for the sauce and pour the remaining batter over the blueberries. Bake for 25–35 minutes, or until a toothpick inserted in the center comes out clean.

5. While the cake is baking, make the lemonade sauce: Place the reserved ½ cup of batter in a medium saucepan. Mix the warm water with the lemonade and stir into the batter, combining well. Over medium heat, cook and stir until the sauce is thick and bubbling. Remove from the heat and stir in the butter.

6. Cut the cake into serving pieces. Place each piece on an individual plate and pour the sauce over it. Garnish with blueberries and a mint sprig. Serve hot or cold.

SERVES 6

For the cake:
¾ CUP SHORTENING (OR A COMBINATION OF SHORTENING AND BUTTER OR MARGARINE)
¾ CUP SUGAR
2 EGGS
¼ TEASPOON LEMON EXTRACT
2 TEASPOONS NEWMAN'S OWN OLD FASHIONED ROADSIDE VIRGIN LEMONADE OR YOUR FAVORITE
2 CUPS FLOUR
1¼ TEASPOONS BAKING POWDER
¼ TEASPOON SALT
½ CUP MILK
2 CUPS FRESH OR FROZEN BLUEBERRIES

For the lemonade sauce:
½ CUP WARM WATER
1½ CUPS NEWMAN'S OWN OLD FASHIONED ROADSIDE VIRGIN LEMONADE OR YOUR FAVORITE
1½ TABLESPOONS BUTTER
FRESH BLUEBERRIES AND MINT SPRIGS FOR GARNISH

Whipped Cream–Filled Banana Cake

1½ CUPS SUGAR

1 STICK (8 TABLESPOONS) BUTTER, SOFTENED

4 BANANAS, MASHED

4 EGGS, LIGHTLY BEATEN

¼ CUP MILK

4 TEASPOONS BAKING SODA

2 CUPS FLOUR

1 PINT COLD HEAVY CREAM

SUGAR TO TASTE

COCOA TO TASTE

Lightly sweetened whipped cream makes a perfect foil for the rich banana flavor of this cake. To get the maximum volume from the cream, be sure that the bowl, beaters, and cream are all chilled.

1. Preheat the oven to 350°F. Grease and flour two 8½-inch square cake pans.

2. In a large bowl, beat together the sugar and butter on medium-high speed of an electric mixer until light and fluffy. Add the bananas and eggs in 2 or 3 batches, beating well after each addition.

3. In a small saucepan or the microwave, bring the milk to a boil. Dissolve the baking soda in it. Add the milk to the banana mixture. Stir in the flour until just blended.

4. Pour into the prepared cake pans and bake for 20–30 minutes, until the top is browned and the center springs back when touched. Remove from the oven and cool on a rack.

5. When the cake is cool, whip the cream until soft peaks form. Add sugar and cocoa to taste. Frost the cake with the cream, spreading it between the layers and over the cake. Sprinkle cocoa on top.

SERVES 10–12

Whoopi Goldberg's Classic American Carrot Cake with a Twist

Toffee-coated macadamia nuts add crunch to this moist carrot cake with traditional cream cheese icing.

1. Preheat the oven to 350°F. Grease a 9½ × 4½-inch tube pan with vegetable oil and flour lightly. Or use two 9-inch round cake pans.

2. To MAKE THE CAKE: In a large bowl, combine the flour, baking powder, baking soda, salt, cinnamon, and sugar. Stir to mix well.

3. Add the oil and beat with a wooden spoon. Add the eggs, one at a time, beating well after each addition.

4. Add the carrots, pineapple, and nuts, blending thoroughly.

5. Pour the batter into the prepared tube pan and bake for 1½ hours, or until a toothpick inserted in the center comes out clean. If you use the 9-inch cake pans, the baking time will be 35–40 minutes. Remove from the oven and cool in the pan on a rack for 5 minutes. Turn the cake out onto the rack and let cool completely.

6. To MAKE THE FROSTING: Beat the margarine and cream cheese with an electric mixer for about 3 minutes or until just smooth. Gradually add the powdered sugar and vanilla and orange extracts, beating until completely blended. If the icing seems too thick, beat in a little milk. Spread evenly over the top of the cake.

SERVES 12–16

Whoopi Goldberg and Frank Langella performing Little Miss Muffett with a camper/garden creature

For the cake:
2 CUPS FLOUR
2 TEASPOONS BAKING POWDER
1½ TEASPOONS BAKING SODA
1½ TEASPOONS SALT
1½ TEASPOONS GROUND CINNAMON
1½ CUPS SUGAR
1½ CUPS MILD-FLAVORED
   VEGETABLE OIL
4 EGGS
2 CUPS FINELY SHREDDED CARROTS
ONE 8½-OUNCE CAN CRUSHED
   PINEAPPLE, DRAINED
6 OUNCES TOFFEE-COATED
   MACADAMIA NUTS, FINELY
   CHOPPED

For the frosting:
1 STICK (8 TABLESPOONS) MARGARINE,
   SOFTENED
ONE 8-OUNCE PACKAGE CREAM CHEESE
1 POUND POWDERED SUGAR, SIFTED
½ TEASPOON VANILLA EXTRACT
½ TEASPOON ORANGE EXTRACT

Dad's Favorite Chocolate-Orange Angel Food Cake

THREE 1.2-OUNCE NEWMAN'S OWN
   ORGANIC DARK ORANGE
   CHOCOLATE BARS, OR 4 OUNCES
   ORANGE-FLAVORED DARK
   CHOCOLATE
12 EGG WHITES
1 CUP FLOUR
1¼ CUPS SUGAR (¼ CUP SIFTED WITH
   THE DRY INGREDIENTS, THE REST
   FOLDED INTO THE EGG WHITES)
½ TEASPOON SALT
1 TABLESPOON LEMON JUICE
3 TEASPOONS VANILLA EXTRACT
1 TABLESPOON GRATED OR FINELY
   CHOPPED ORANGE RIND

Nell Newman, Paul's daughter, developed this low-fat cake, which is light and airy, yet moist and richly flavored. It is delicious on its own or when topped with strawberries and whipped cream.

If you like to work barehanded, separate the eggs by breaking them, one at a time, into one very clean hand and letting the white dribble through your fingers into a bowl. Use the same bare hand (with the egg white washed off) to fold the dry ingredients into the beaten egg whites. Keep your fingers spread and use a gentle lifting motion. You will need a 10 × 4-inch tube pan, either a traditional angel food pan with little legs, or a regular tube pan. Turn the cake pan upside down immediately after removing from the oven, or it will fall. Stand the pan on its legs or raise it above the tabletop by setting the tube over a bottle or supporting the rim of the pan on four glasses or cans.

1. Preheat the oven to 350°F. Make sure your 10 × 4-inch tube pan is perfectly clean, dry, and free of grease.

2. Grate the chocolate bars on the fine holes of a cheese grater (not the teeny holes of a citrus grater).

3. Separate the eggs, reserving the yolks for another use. Let the egg whites come to room temperature, about 15 minutes.

4. Sift the flour, ¼ cup of sugar, and salt onto a piece of waxed paper. Sift the dry ingredients together twice more, three times in all.

5. Beat the egg whites until frothy. Add the lemon juice and continue beating. Sprinkle the remaining sugar, ¼ cup at a time, over the egg whites and continue beating at medium speed until the egg whites are glossy and form soft peaks that bend over at the top. Do not overbeat, or the egg whites will lose their volume.

6. Sift ¼ cup of the dry ingredients over the whites and fold into the egg whites. Gently stir in the vanilla extract and orange rind. Alternately fold in the chocolate and remaining dry ingredients, working in small batches, until just incorporated.

7. Pour the batter into the tube pan and bake for 45 minutes, until the top is lightly browned. A knife inserted in the center of the cake should come out clean.

8. Remove from the oven and invert the pan. Allow the cake to cool for 30–45 minutes. Run a knife around the edges of the pan and the tube to loosen the cake.

SERVES 8–10

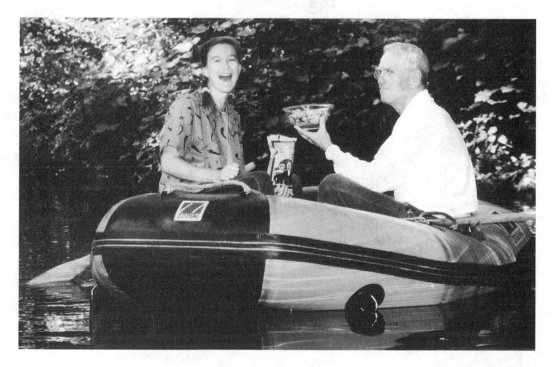

Nell and Dad

Lunch Box Specials

If you've run out of ideas for your lunch box, try some of these inspired combinations.

Jerry Stiller's Roasted Turkey Breast (page 50) sandwich on rye bread with pickles, yellow mustard, iceberg lettuce, tomatoes, and low-fat cheddar cheese
Apple or grapes
Whoopi Goldberg's Classic American Carrot Cake with a Twist (page 113)

Turkey, bacon, lettuce, and tomato sandwich on rye with honey mustard or mayonnaise, Monterey Jack cheese, and avocado slices (optional)
Raw baby carrots
Michael Bolton's White Chocolate Brownie (page 110)

Eggstraordinary Egg Salad (page 34) sandwiches on whole wheat bread with iceberg lettuce and turkey bacon (optional)
Pickled cucumbers
Peanut Butter Chocolate Chip Cookies (page 108)

Sausage Sandwiches (page 25)
Celery and carrot sticks
Your favorite cookie

Triple-Threat Meat Loaf (page 51) sandwiches on a crusty roll with ketchup
or barbecue sauce
Corn chips or tortilla chips
Apple or pear

★ ★ ★

Lemonade Chicken Wings (page 44; don't forget to include a towelette)
Rice cakes
Raisin-Walnut Snack Cake (page 95)

★ ★ ★

Cold southern-fried chicken
Sweet Corn Bread (page 88)
Carrot strips

★ ★ ★

Ants on a Tree (page 87)
Sweet and Savory Cheddar Muffins (page 93)
Apple slices
Colonel Pop's Fun Friday Popcorn Pops (page 97)

★ ★ ★

Paul's Pocketful o' Peas (page 30)
Pear
Rosemary Clooney's Two-Fisted Chocolate Chip Cookies (page 107)

★ ★ ★

Nut butter (almond, cashew, or peanut) on whole wheat or sourdough bread
with chopped celery
Grapes
Caramel-flavored mini rice cakes

Chicken breast rolled in a flour tortilla (whole wheat if possible) with Monterey Jack
cheese, mustard, and sprouts (if you can get away with it)
Nacho-flavored corn chips
Newman's Very Own Lemon Blueberry Cake (without the Lemon Sauce;
(page 111)

Ham and cheese rolled in flat bread or tortilla with mustard and shredded lettuce
Pickle spears
Your favorite oatmeal raisin cookie

A gala finale

I thank God that I have both legs—
   to limp is no disgrace.
Although I can't be number one,
   I can still run the race.
It's not what you can't do
   that makes you who you are,
but what you <u>can</u> do
   that shines the morning star.

Sue,
camper

Index

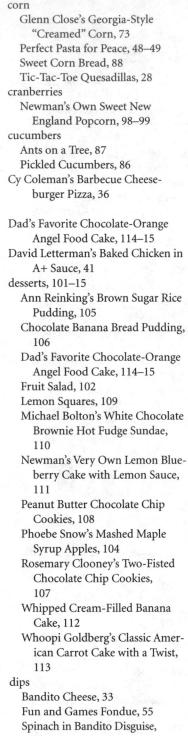

Metric Equivalencies

Liquid and Dry Measure Equivalencies

Customary	Metric
¼ teaspoon	1.25 milliliters
½ teaspoon	2.5 milliliters
1 teaspoon	5 milliliters
1 tablespoon	15 milliliters
1 fluid ounce	30 milliliters
¼ cup	60 milliliters
⅓ cup	80 milliliters
½ cup	120 milliliters
1 cup	240 milliliters
1 pint (2 cups)	480 milliliters
1 quart (4 cups, 32 ounces)	960 milliliters (.96 liters)
1 gallon (4 quarts)	3.84 liters
1 ounce (by weight)	28 grams
¼ pound (4 ounces)	114 grams
1 pound (16 ounces)	454 grams
2.2 pounds	1 kilogram (1000 grams)

Oven Temperature Equivalencies

Description	Fahrenheit	Celsius
Cool	200	90
Very slow	250	120
Slow	300–325	150–160
Moderately slow	325–350	160–180
Moderate	350–375	180–190
Moderately hot	375–400	190–200
Hot	400–450	200–230
Very Hot	450–500	230–260

About the Authors

PAUL NEWMAN

Paul Newman is probably best known for his spectacularly successful food conglomerate. In addition to giving the profits to charity, he also ran Frank Sinatra out of the spaghetti sauce business. On the downside, Newman's spaghetti sauce is outgrossing his films.

He graduated from Kenyon College and in the process begat a laundry business that was the only student-run enterprise on Main Street. Yale University later awarded him an Honorary Doctorate of Humane Letters for unknown reasons.

He has won four Sports Car Club of America National Championships and is listed in the *Guinness Book of World Records* as the oldest driver (seventy) to win a professionally sanctioned race (the 24-hour Daytona, 1995).

He is married to the best actress on the planet, was number 19 on Nixon's enemy list, and, purely by accident, has appeared in fifty-one films and four Broadway plays.

He is generally considered by professionals to be the worst fisherman on the East Coast.

A. E. HOTCHNER

A. E. Hotchner has written twelve books and six plays, and in one way or another, food has found its way into all of them. In *Papa Hemingway,* which was published in twenty-six languages in thirty-eight countries, there are vivid descriptions of memorable meals with Hemingway and dishes that Hemingway particularly liked.

Hotch has also graphically described meals in some of his novels, most recently in *Louisiana Purchase.* In an earlier book, *King of the Hill,* Hotch depicted a summer of his life when he was twelve; there was no food on the table, and to assuage his hunger he sometimes cut food ads from magazines and ate them.